# Heart of Africa

The Story of an Adventurer

# Heart of Africa

The Story of an Adventurer

Frederick Moir

Edited by Ian M. Thomson

James McIntyre Publishing Ltd

This Edition Copyright 2001 Ian Thomson

This new edition first published in Great Britain by
James McIntyre Publishing Ltd
36 West Bank, Carlton
Goole
DN14 9PZ

First Published in Great Britain by
Hodder & Stoughton in 1923

ISBN 09540 06003

All rights reserved. No part of this publication may be reproduced, stored in a retreival system or transmitted in any form or by any means electronic, electrostatic, magnetic tape, mechanical photocopying, recording or otherwise, without prior permission of the publishers.

Printed and bound in Great Britain by
Viking Press Northern Ltd

*About the Author:*

Frederick Moir was born in Edinburgh in 1852. He studied Botany and Natural History at Edinburgh University. He moved to London in the 1870's taking on various commercial postions. In 1877 he went to Africa along with his brother. He returned to Scotland in 1892. Became the Company Secretary for the Africa lakes Company and remained on the board for many years. He died in November 1939, his elder brother survived him by one year.

*About the Editor:*

Ian Thomson graduated from Lancaster University in 1983 with a History degree. He has worked in publishing ever since. The book which 'Heart of Africa' is based on was originally owned by his Grandmother who lived and worked in Malawi in the 1920's and 1930's. His Grandfather was a storeman and later a General Merchant, probably with the Africa Lakes Company and unfortunately he died of Malaria in 1937.

*Acknowledgements:*
The editor would like to thank his mother Margery Thomson for giving him the inspiration, his wife for proof reading and constructive critiscm and finally Don McKenzie at African Lakes, for his help and support.

*Cover Photograph:*
The Author in 1885

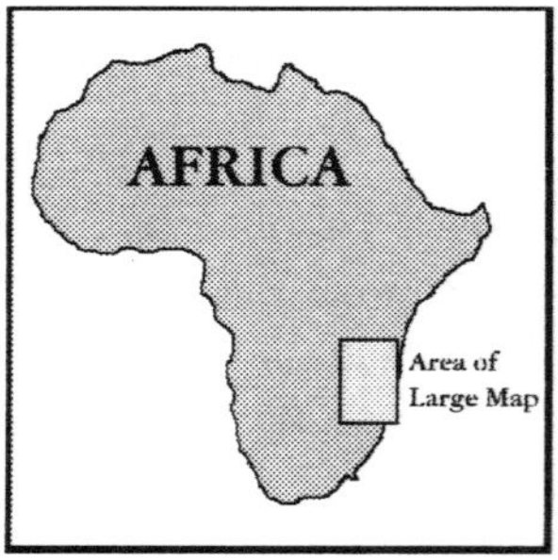
AFRICA
Area of Large Map

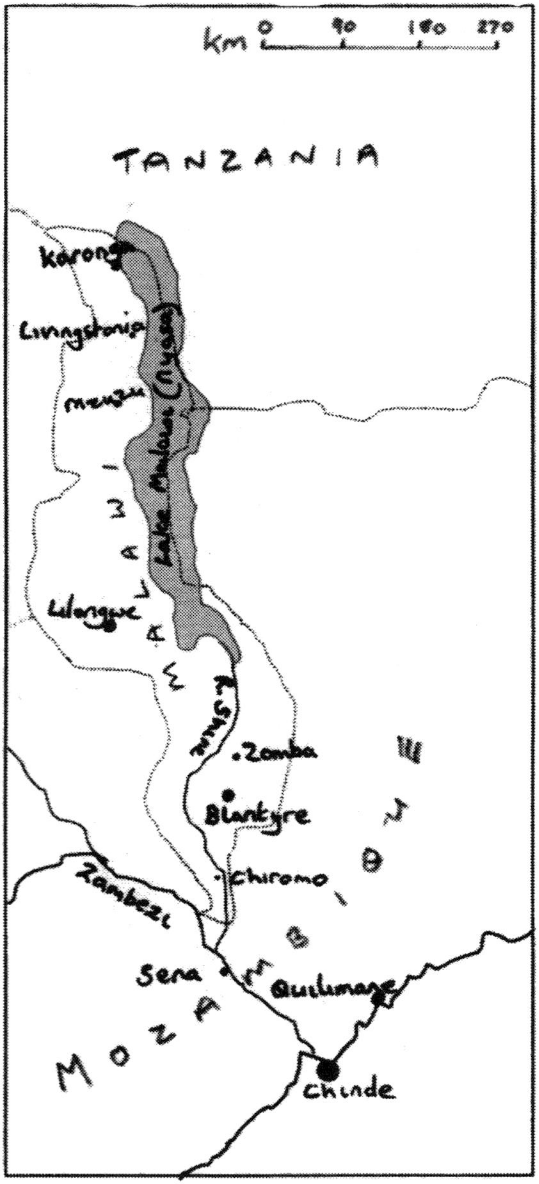
km 0 90 180 270
TANZANIA
Karonga
Livingstonia
Mzuzu
MALAWI
Lake Malawi (Nyasa)
Lilongwe
R. Shire
Zomba
Blantyre
Chiromo
Zambezi
Sena
Quilimane
Chinde
MOZAMBIQUE

# Contents

| | | |
|---|---|---|
| **Chapter I** | How We Came to be Pioneers/t | 5 |
| **Chapter II** | Forming the Company | 11 |
| **Chapter III** | Early Difficulties | 17 |
| **Chapter IV** | Among the Wild Angoni | 23 |
| **Chapter V** | The Lady Nyasa Goes Upriver | 33 |
| **Chapter VI** | Weird Ivory Palavers | 41 |
| **Chapter VII** | Establishing Headquarters | 49 |
| **Chapter VIII** | A Poisin Ordeal | 57 |
| **Chapter IX** | Cutting the Slave-Routes | 65 |
| **Chapter X** | Routed by a Hippo | 71 |
| **Chapter XI** | Transporting a Steamer | 79 |
| **Chapter XII** | The Slave Caravan | 85 |
| **Chapter XIII** | A Wonderful Country | 89 |
| **Chapter XIV** | The Crocodiles Victim | 95 |
| **Chapter XV** | My First Elephant | 99 |
| **Chapter XVI** | A Big Bag | 105 |
| **Chapter XVII** | Taming Young Elephants | 111 |
| **Chapter XVIII** | Smaller Game | 117 |
| **Chapter XIX** | A Rebellion | 119 |
| **Chapter XX** | An Invasion and Murder | 127 |
| **Chapter XXI** | The Slave Traders Attack Us | 133 |
| **Chapter XXII** | Wounded | 141 |
| **Chapter XXIII** | How the War Ended | 147 |
| **Chapter XXIV** | Trading Scenes in Ujiji | 153 |
| **Chapter XXV** | A Narrow Escape From Natives | 165 |
| | Prologue | 175 |

# Introduction

The history of British involvement in Africa is described in modem day parlance as being one of colonisation and exploitation. During the mid to latter part of the 19th Century Africa was opened up and was now seen as a new territory for European expansion and domination.

For the British, the quest for territory was dominated by two commercial operations. There was Sir William Mackinnon and his British Central African Company based around modern day Kenya and Uganda and in the south was Cecil Rhodes and the British South Africa Company. Sandwiched between the two was Portuguese East Africa (now Mozambique), German East Africa (Tanzania) and a small area bordering the vast expanse of Lake Nyasa. This area known as Nyasaland (modern day Malawi) was extensively visited by David Livingstone in the 1850's and was the centre of the slave trade in Central East Africa.

Here a small group of mainly Scottish businessmen and missionaries set up The Africa lakes Company. The companies avowed aims were the expansion of trade with the natives, the abolition of the slave trade and for the missionary element, the bringing of Christianity to the area. The watchword of the company was, even in those days of colonisation and exploitation, 'Africa for the Africans'. This book is the first hand account of one of the founding managers of this company.

To understand and enjoy this book to its fullest, caveats must be set. It must be remembered that the book, albeit written in the 1920's, was the recollection of one man, who viewed his work in Africa as being on a purely philanthropic basis. He himself was critical of the way in later years Europeans settled in Africa, building fantastically large farms and ranches, taking the livelihood away from local farmers who in turn were forced to work on these ranches as lowly farmhands in order to survive. It was this mass settlement of Europeans into the agricultural economies which caused many of the pre-independence conflicts and we can see the results now in Zimbabwe. For the Frederick Moir of the book, you get the feeling that such actions would have been an anathema. His aim of setting up trading operations with the indigenous peoples was not only to benefit the company and the native traders, but also to provide alternatives to slavery and forced labour and not for personal wealth.

His views on the local wild animal population, which to modern eyes would lead him open to mass protests, were at the time the absolute norm. Africa in the 1870's was not confining its beasts to National Parks, the Elephant population was so large that to most they were regarded as merely pests. The killing of elephants for their meat and ivory was for many the culling of a bothersome animal. Indeed for this area of Africa, ivory was the only 'economical' crop which was suitable for export. As Moir details the killing of the elephants you will notice how every part of the animal is used by the locals once the ivory has been removed, from the skin of the ears to the hairs on the tail nothing is wasted. This attitude is a long way from the sad sight of dead elephants lying, shot for nothing but their ivory.

In his relationship with the local peoples and the Arab slave traders, you are struck by his conciliatory and friendly manner. Obviously the Africa Company did not have the clout of Cecil Rhodes or Mackinnon, but their policy of negotiation and partnership seemed, initially, to have had the desired effect. To put this into perspective, at the same time as Moir was handling delicate negotiations with the Angoni Zulu peoples, resulting in trade agreements. A thousand or so miles to the south, the British Army were fighting the Zulus at Islandewande and Rorkes Drift.

It must be remembered that this is an autobiography and there is an absence of details of mistakes and errors of judgement, of which there must have been some, as in every life. You cannot help but feel that had his attitude and philosophy towards Africa prevailed, as opposed to the mass settlement and exploitation, perhaps the history of this vast continent in the 20th Century may have been less troubled.

# Chapter 1

**HOW WE CAME TO BE PIONEERS**

The Africa Lakes Company was founded in response to the call of David Livingstone, who declared that two conditions were essential for the abolition of the terrible slave-trade in the Dark Continent - Christianity and legitimate commerce.

Mission work had begun at various points, but no systematic endeavour had been made to providethe commerce until my brother and I undertook the task. It may interest readers to know of something of the men who pioneered the opening of inland Africa to trade, and some of the influences which had fitted them for what they came to do.

My brother (John William) and I (Frederick Lewis Maitland Moir) were born in Edinburgh in 1851 and 1852 respectively. We were always close companions and trusted friends. John, as a boy, was a born leader and fond of investigation, but being short-sighted he, not unnaturally, met with more than his share of accidents. While opening a gate he cut the pupil of his right eye with a knife he had in his right hand, permanently damaging it. He got his fingers crushed in the hay-chopper in our stable loft, "blew up" his face with gunpowder and damaged another finger while woodturning, all within a comparatively short time. If he thought a thing should be done, he would try to do it. I made a good second, and was usually hany at repairing damage and carrying on the ventures.

We had many hobbies, and set up a bookbinding press and guillotine, turning out what we considered very well bound books. Both of us were fond of repairing clocks, and I remember a derelict one, which we mended and fitted up with a toy pistol so that it fired and emptied shot into a basin as a morning alarm.

This particular hobby stood in good stead om many occasions in Africa and any broken watch or clock in the countryside usually found its way to our quarters. Once my brother had a watch completely dismantled when the mail arrived, he jumped up eagerly, upset the table, and that watch was never wound again.

We were both fond of rowing and swimming, always most useful accomplishments, but specially so for travellers. I was particularly fond of shooting, and won the Duke of Hamilton's Challenge Cup in the Queen's Edinburgh Rifles. All this training was invaluable in the early days in Africa.

Our father was Dr. John Moir, a well known physician in Edinburgh. His father, a naval surgeon, was captured during the Napoleonic wars and was kept a prisoner on parole for seven years in the now famous Verdun. There his wife, who managed to get into France by acting as a lady's maid to a General's wfe, joined him and there our father was born. In fact he spoke French for the first five years of his life.

Our mother was Margaret Loisa Heriot Maitland of Ramornie, Fife. It was her uncle, Admiral Sir Frederick Lewis

Maitland, to whom Napoleon surrendered on H.M.S. Belerophon.

On leaving school, we went to Switzerland and Germany for two years, acquiring a knowledge of French and German, which later turned out to be of great use on the African coast and enabled us more easily to learn Portuguese.

Returning to Edinburgh, we entered the University, where we studied Botany and natural History. On Saturday forenoons, at the School of Arts, we learned carpentry and woodturning.

We began our business training in a chartered accountant's office, after which John entered a timber merchant's and I a corn factor's office, both in Leith. Thence John proceeded to London, to an Indian merchant's office and thereafter the office of the Union Insurance Society of Canton. I followed, working several yearswith the same Indian mrechant,later I opened the first large cycle agency in in the city of London, to which a factory was added later.

Like our parents we were interested both in church and in missions and engaged in work in Edinburgh and also with the Regent Square Church in London.

It was while we were thus comfortably situated at home, with good prospects that John,as usual the leader, was fired by Dr. Livingstone's appeal to men to lend a hand in the abolition of the slave-trade and the opening up of a very dark continent to civilisation.

In 1877, the interior of Africa was very little known and when for a moment the curtain was lifted, the picture was very black indeed. Slavery, although abolished throughout British dominins, was still rampant on the East Coast. Especially in those lands claimed by the Sultan of Zanzibar and in Portuguese possessions. Ivory was almost the only product that would bear the cost of transportation from the interior and the only known economical means of transporting it was the slave-gang.

Even if missionaries succeeded in implanting Christain ideals into the natives, there could be little hope of them advancing in civilisation and self-support unless they had some means of disposing of their raw materials and the fruits of their industry. For thus only would they be able to settle in self-supporting communities and supply themselves with European goods and clothing. Obviously the pressing needs were to provide mechanical transport in order to dispense with the necessity of slave-labour. Then to give paid employment to those who were willing to work, and to provide a market where the native could dispose of his produce in exchange for European manufactures.

The known land routes were rendered difficult and dangerous by long waterless stretches and the rivers, which might have been expected to be the natural highways into the interior, were blocked by waterfalls. Africa may be divided into three spheres of altitude; the coastal plains, navigable from the seaboard, the intermediate levels and the high plateux. Two sets of waterfall on great rivers mark the descent from one level to the next.

On the Congo, the intermediate plateau is only ninety miles from the coast there the Stanley Falls, extending over one hundred and seventy miles, effectively block navigation. The deadly climate caused by an equatorial luxuriant vegetation, the breeding ground for mosquitoes and the steep broken hill country along the falls, explain why the Congo remained so long closed.

On the Zambesi, the coastal plains extended much farther so that navigation was possible for three hundred miles. To the Kebrabassa rapids to the west of Tete and then to the Murchison Falls on the Shire River, an affluent of the Zambesi from the north. In this case the chief obstacles were the sandbars at the mouths of the Zambasi, the unhealthy delta fringed with mangrove swamps and the deadly climate of the long low-lying valley of the Zambesi. Perhaps the chief obstacle was the prior occupation for a long period of parts of the Zambesi valley by the Portuguese and the very unsatisfactory relations existing between them and the native tribes farther inland.

So much difficulty was experienced in reaching Lake Nyasa through Portuguese possessions that Thomas Fowell Buxton and Sir William Mackinnon determined to make a road to the lake. By taking a route to the north of Portuguese influence, it would be clear of political and fiscal difficulties as well as the antagonism of the half-castes and natives on the Zambesi route.

It was as unpaid volunteers on this road that my brother and I gained our first experience of East Africa and began our tropical training.

After consultation with Sir William Mackinnon, we determined, if we were allowed to go out together, that we would give up our home employments and prospects and devote our lives to Africa. Our offer was accepted, we settled our affairs at home and started for Zanzibar in May 1877.

Dr. (later Sir) John Kirk [1] was deeply interested in the new British venture, and lent it his powerful influence. He assisted in equiping the expedition, introduced its members to the Sultan, and procured from the latter the use of his little steamer, The Deerhound, to carry us to our point of departure on the mainland.

The expedition was led for the first months by Mr. W. Mayes, a sergeant of Engineers with Indian and Persian experience. Starting from Dar-Es-Salaam, then almost unknown but later the headquarters of the German East African Government, we constructed a road for about twenty miles. First we built through cocoanut plantations and then set through jungle and forest. We spent a wet season in the jungle, a fitting apprenticeship for the hardsips of life in Africa.

Although this road was not proceeded with , our work on it gave us valuable experience in dealing and trading with natives and Arabs. We also learnt the Swahili language, which is a lingua franca throughout East Africa. Returning to Scotland in the early summer of 1878, we decided to carry out a plan of approach by the Zambesi route, notwithstanding the difficulties to be expected by any foreigner endeavouring to open up the Portuguese hinterland to trade.

---

Notes:

1 Dr Sir John Kirk (1832 -1922). After service in the Crimea War, he became the chief officer in Dr Livingstone's 1853 expedition to Central Africa. Later in 1886 he was appointed Consul General and Her Majesty's agent to Zanzibar. Here he stayed until 1887 when he retired from consular service.

# Chapter II

**FORMING THE COMPANY**

The events described at the close of the last chapter were a valuable experience, and the knowledge gained then of tradingand our previous knowledge of leading British manufacturers and merchants accustomed to supplying Indian markets, helped us with the new project, namely a new expedition to Lake Nyasa with Lake Tanganyika also in view. Business friends in London supported the venture and negotiations were entered into with manufacturers and produce-brokers, many connections being formed which have remained unbroken to this day.

At this juncture several influential men in Glasgow, including many of the principal promoters and supporters of the Livingstonia Mission of the Free Church, suggested the formation of a Scottish company to co-operate in the work and to form the company we had in mind.

Amongst those who took a leading part in promoting the interests of the concern were; Mr. James Stevenson of Hailie, Largs, a keen geographer and student of Government reports, who was elected chairman and continued so to act until his death twenty-five years later; Mr John Stephen, partner of Alexander Stephen & Sons, the well known shipbuilders of Govan, who for the long period of thirty five years contributed his practical knowledge of steamers and exercised his shrewd business sense and determination on behalf of the enterprise; and finally Mr James Young of Kelly, the well-known chemist and pioneer of Shale Oil Industry.

The company which, to acknowledge the inspiration derived from the great explorer, was called the Livingstonia Central Africa Company Limited. It was formed on the 21st of June 1878 and my brother and I were appointed joint managers.

The fundamental idea was to reach thr heart of Africa by transport on the rivers and lakes and porterages where these were required between the navigable reaches.

The nominal capital was £20,000 in shares of £500 each. Of this, £12,000 was subscribed in about equal parts by ourselves, friends and by the directors, £7,200 being called up by the end of 1878. The capital and the personnel were eventually found to be much to small for the large operations planned by the company.

We, as the joint-managers, were 'to superintend the route between Quilimane on the East Coast via Blantyre and Lake Nyasa, to circumnavigate that lake and to start a branch line up the Zambesi to Tete and other lines (on to Lake Tanganyika) as they might open up.' We were also ' to carry traffic with the natives, establish depots, assist in exploration and keep regular books'.

When it is remembered that geographical expeditions to reach and explore territories similarly distant often cost £25,000 to £30,000, the modesty of the capitalisation of the Company in relation to its ambitious permanent program would become apparent.

Not only had we to purchase the river steamer, supply boats and craft for smaller waterway, bulid and equip stations and provide goods for Europeans and natives, we had also to keep open communications as regularly and frequently as possible for mails and goods over the long broken waterways between the coast and Lake Nyasa.

We chose as our first assistants; Robert Henderson, engineer, Robert Reid, ship's carpenter and Robert Dent, sailor. A light draught steamer, built by Yarrow & Co. was delivered to us in paltes and frames for re-erection abroad. Trading goods and stores in loads and suitably packed for inland transport were got ready.

In August 1878 our little party of five embarked on the Union Castle steamer 'German', which made a record trip, for the time, of twenty days to the Cape. There we transhipped into the small steamer 'Natal' and after a stormy passage round the Cape we approached our destination about a fortnight later.

The coast being very flat and low, it was difficult to make out the Quilimine or Kwakwa River, but certain palm trees were sighted, and guided by beacons on shore we crossed the bar and entered the estuary. The coast-line was composed of rolling hillocks of sand washed up by the great waves of the Indian Ocean. The banks of the river were covered by beautiful green trees and shrubs, the water reaching to the base of the trees, indeed, wherever there was an opening in the undergrowth, one could see that the high tide had overflowed the banks so that not only the numerous deep creeks but also large tracts of wooded country were submerged.   Hippopotami could be seen, curlews, cormorants, divers of various kinds alarmed by the steamer, circled in the air or retreated before it. A bend in the river disclosed Quilimane, with a number of large, red-tiled houses flanking a main street and a small church occuping the foreground. So far, the river and the town were charming. We seemed to be in a tropical paradise.

As the steamer came to anchor we fired a gun and awaited the arrival of the Portuguese officials. After some delay the Custom House officers, with much gold lace and fluttering of Portuguese flags, arrived in boats manned by stalwart natives. The British Vice-Consul, Senhor Jose Nunes, a Portuguese friend of Livingstone, gave us acordial welcome and an invitation to stay under his care. He also assisted us to pass our large consignment of goods through the Custom House.

What a change when the tide had ebbed! A stretch of several hundred feet of slimy mud lay before the town. Deep cuttings, which intersected the town at intervals and carried off the water from swamps behind, were muddy and obnoxious to eye and nose. The mangrove trees, which bordered the river as we came up were seen to be rooted in the same black ooze, which, under the rays of the tropical sun, sent forth pestilential vapours. It was this fringe of malarial swamp ( found in the deltas of almost all tropical rivers) which had been so great a barrier against the exploration and colonisation of the interior. Until we established regular steam communication, a delay was necessary for all newcomers before starting inland and that delay not only laid many down with fever but also sowed the germs of illness to come.

It was not a lifeless stretch of mud. If it were approached quietly, hundreds of little crabs, three or four inches long of various colours, could be seen hard at work. They plunged into holes, whence, after some digging, they emerged with two little pellets of mud, which they carried some distance, laid them down and then went back to dig. Where the water touched the bank were dozens of lively fish, two or four inches long, shaped much like the blennies found at home pools. They used their fins as rudimentary legs, by means of which they paddled at a great rate across the mud after the receding tide. In the sea itself, on sandy beaches, prawns of magnificent size and flavour were found in great quantities.

On the Kwakwa, the tide, which has a rise and fall of between sixteen to eighteen feet at spring tides, runs far inland up the river. In these tidal waters the banks are ofetn composed of oozy mud, which at times makes landing during low water practically impossible. The town of Quilimane had been built at a less muddy point and at several places the river bank was fairly hard and sandy.

We selected one of these places for the building of our first steamer, 'The Lady Nyasa', and erected a low wooden staging. It was planned so that at the highest spring tides, the hull when plated, would float off. At neap tides the water did not reach the hull or the bank below it. But as the spring tide approached, work on the hull had to be suspended during high water. As the steamer, sixty feet long by twelve feet broad, was flat-bottomed in order to float on as little water as possible, the riveters had to lie on boards or matting on the mud.

In order that she might be finished before next spring tides all, managers included, lent a hand at this very dirty job. Great was the astonishment of the Portuguese to see white men, and especially the managers, working along with the natives.

We had engaged some natives to help in building the steamer. At first all communications had to be done in signs, but gradually we learned a few Portuguese words and the natives picked up some of the spiciest Govan dialect. Above the din of riveting hammers one could hear a native holder-on yelling "Aw richt". One native, who remained years in the service, was always known by the nameof "Aw richt", on account of his delicious pronunciation.

After weeks of hard work the hull was completed, the engines fitted up and the light cabin built. Every difficulty had been surmounted, and 'The Lady Nyasa' was ready for work. The natives were at last satisfied that the white man could make iron float and our Portuguese friends were hardly less astonished at the result of our work. The elite of the town came to enjoy the trial trip. The Governor and officials, Portuguese, Dutch and French watched with interest as the engines began to move. The little cockle-shell, drawing a foot of water, paddled downstream towards a bar. All went well till we had to cross the river. Some spray raised by the sea breezes came on board and our passengers, seeking shelter, crowded to leeward and almost over balanced 'her ladyship'. This danger having been averted, the galley did its best to provide luncheon. We carried no alcoholic liquor, but drew on stores for effervescing drinks, so great was the demand that our supplies failed. Not to be daunted, the house-boys made up the defeciency by drawing on our supply of Eno's Fruit Salt! This was a case of drinking healths with a vengeance!

The afternoon breezes made steering difficult for so light a vessel carrying considerable top-hamper, but the trial ended successfully.

# Chapter III

### EARLY DIFFICULTIES

The conditions in the vast district which we intended to open up to civilised trade were at this time of the most unpromising character.

The Portuguese had taken possession of the East Coast to search for gold. They occupied only three or four towns on the coast-line and two stations inland, namely Sena and Tete on the Zambesi River. They also made a general claim to the whole continent as far as the Atlantic Ocean, though most of the hinterland was unknown to them and they had never visited it. They have never been a successful colonising power. Being a poor nation, they could not, or would not, apy their officials and soldiers adequately. Hence arose the incentivefor both to resort to all sorts of illegal impositions in order to eke out their incomes. The natives were taxed, but not at so much per head. The Government farmed out districts by auction to Portuguese subjects and officers, who paid as little as £60 per annum, but were reputed to have squeezed £1,000 or more from the people in produce and labour. Good as might be the codified laws and the intentions in Lisbon, such a system, corrupt to the core, could not but lead to poverty, hatred and war.

And so it did. Just before we arrived, there had been one of the periodic risings against the Portuguese, possibly on account of some atrocious barbarity of a black underling, and a war of retaliation took place. One tribe was induced to side with the Portuguese. The rebels were defeated and grim accounts reached us of natives being tortured, killed and disembowelled 'pour encourager les autres'. The various half-caste Portuguese on the Zambesi kept large bands of armed natives about them and were practically independent, levying tolls on all merchandise (private or Government) passing up the Tete.

Sena was annually visited by Landeens, a Zulu tribe, and to save trouble, the Portuguese paid them a yearly sum and were left in comparative peace.

In the country farther inland, practically untouched by the Portuguese, there were feuds between the Sena men and the Makolo and consequently there were wars on the frontiers. The original inhabitants of the Shire Highlands, the Manganja tribe, had been driven from much of their country by the Wayao or Ajawa and Machinga from the north, who in turn had been forced to move onwards by the Magwangwara (of Zulu origin). Later from the south, the Makololo were moving forward, causing war and feud as they went. At Blantyre, round the missionwhich had been established in the preceding year, there was somewhat of the 'Pax Britannica'. But moral suasion, while effective on those near enough to be influenced by the Mission, had little result on outlying tribes whose chiefs made war on those who had congregated round the British. On the west of Nyasa there was constant strife between the Angoni (Zulu) and the Atonga, who had been driven from the hills and had settled in great numbers on islands and in swamps on the lake shore. This was complicated and encouraged by the presence at Kota Kota and elsewhere of Arabs who were always ready to buy slaves and to ferment wars, even when they were not raiding on their own account.

The country to the north of Nyasa and towards Tanganyika was still unexplored, though we ascertained later that similar wars and feuds were taking place there. On the plateau the tribes were broken up into villages, with little common coherence and could offer no effective resistance to the bands of Awemba from the south. Villages, even if situated for defence on some angle of a stream or in a swamp, fell an easy prey to a lengthened seige while in the Tanganyika region, again, the Arabs and the Awemba together were desolating whole countries.

Hardly anywhere could one see the ideal African town; industrious, happy and living generously on the abundance that nature provides for the thrifty. The people could be divided into two categories. There were the strong, who could hold their own and live in comparative comfort and who almost invariably used their power to conquer others and take the spoils. Then there were the weak, always on the defensive, liable at any moment to be burned out of house and home and to have their wives and daughters murdered in the fields or carried off as slaves. We were now only beginning to realise the magnitude of the problem ahead of us. What we had to do was:

1. Discover the best method for utilising the river and lake route.
2. Establish a regular mail and goods transport service to Lake Nyasa and beyond.
3. Get in touch and make friends with the natives
4. Foster the production and sale of commodities which would pay for the transport.

5. Induce the natives to engage themselves for paid employment.

The distance over which we had to maintain communication was approximateley that between Glasgow and Marseilles. We had to navigate difficult rivers and negotiate native paths one or two feet wide meandering between villages.

Fortunately, for a large portion of the distance there ran the silver streak of river or lake navigation. But the rivers were sometimes so shallow that a boat drawing more than a foot of water could not pass. Elsewhere there were marshes and blocks of sudd. There were also breaks of three miles and sixty miles, where goods would have to be unshipped and carried on heads of natives these long distances. To reach Tanganyika, over two hundred miles of unknown roadless mountainous country would have to be traversed.

Not a native beyond the coast was able to read or write and all were suspicious of strangers. Instead of requiring to know only English and French, we needed Portuguese, Chagunda, Chinyanja and Chiyao on the actual journeys and other languages for the Lake dwellers. In Quilimane, the British Vice-Consul Nunes and one or two Dutchmen, spoke English fairly well. No one else would even venture even a few words. Several Portuguses and French traders were approachable in French, a few travelled natives knew some words of Swahili, otherwise a language of signs had to be devised.

The Kwakwa was often spoken of as one of the mouths of the Zambesi, the most northerly of the many streams that form its delta. During the greater part of the year there is no connection between them, though near Mopea they approach to within a few miles. But during the rainy season any considerable rise of the Zambesi flooded a low lying channel, the Balambwanda and allowed boats and canoes to pass. Senhor Nunes, the Consul, declared we would be able to reach Quilimane every rainy season.

Our projected route was by boat or canoe four to five days journey up the Kwakwa, then by land transport about three miles to Mazaro on the Zambesi. Thence by our own steamer up the Zambesi and Shire to Katunga, then overland sixty miles past the Murchison Cataracts through Blantyre to Matope and thence by steamer direct to Lake Nyasa.

Until the rainy season brought the usual floods, on which we counted to get our stemer to the Zambesi, we employed her in transporting our cargo as far up the Kwakwa as she could go, whence it was carried farther in small boats and dug-out canoes as far as Marendinny and thence overland about three miles to Mazaro on the Zambesi.

Mysterious deterioration of the steel hull caused by the brackish water added to the difficulties and worries of those in charge. To secure the maximum strength on the lightest possible draft, the hull had been plated with the finest steel sheets, one sixteenth of an inch thick. These were carefully painted, but in shallow riverservice the paint quickly wore off. Within three months of the launch, small, clean, round holes, like the prick of an ordinary pin, made their appearance in the steel and gradually enlarging, called for constant watchfulness and frequent repairs.

Dr. Livingstone in the Zambesi waters had similar troubles and, not unnaturally, though mistakenly, he attributed them to defective materials.

# Chapter IV

### AMONG THE WILD ANGONI

When the steamer was still plying on the Kwakwa awaiting the rise of the river, I proceeded, at the end of 1878, to Blantyre and Lake Nyasa to get in touch with the missions and open trading relations with the natives. My brother remained to supervise operations on the coast and so with one boat and some large canoes hired from the natives, I started on the three week journey up the Zambesi and Shire Rivers to Katunga near the Murchison Cataracts. Here a steep and difficult climb of about ten miles took us onto the Shire Highlands plateau, an undulating country indeed. A walk of fifteen more miles brought us to Blantyre, which then consisted of six small pole and grass cottages, the walls plastered with mud.

The Rev. J. Duff Macdonald, who was in charge of the Church of Scotland Mission, was experiencing considerable difficulty with the chiefs over the many questions incidental to the opening of new settlements. He was also facing the distrust of chiefs hostile to those who had received the missionaries and the ever-present problem of slaves running away from their masters.

The Livingstonia Mission steamer *'Ilala'* having arrived from Lake Nyasa at Matope, we took a thirty five mile tramp thither and started for the Lake. The *'Ilala'* was a screw steamer about fifty feet long, drawing about five feet. The river was broad and deep, anything less than eight feet of water being viewed with concern. But sufficient water was then available at all seasons of the year and for many years after.

Lake Nyasa was a focus of the slave trade. Powerful Arabs had established fortified villages at strategic points. Mponda had his large village on the west side of the river, within a mile or two of the Lake. Here slaves could easily be ferried across the Shire in any weather. On the west side of Nyasa, towards the south, Makanjila was established, also Jumbe at Kota Kota half-way up the Lake. Both had slave dhows which ferried their cargoes to the eastern shore.

The Livingstonia Mission had come to a friendly arrangement with Mponda when establishing its first station at Cape Maclear, the large promontory which projects into the lake from the southern end. Here, protected by two islands, a safe anchorage was available for the '*Ilala*', a necessity for her existence in that lake of storms. The site, owing to undrainable swamps behind the station and the refraction of heat from the rocky hills behind, was found to be unhealthy. Already the graveyard, in the shadow of a great boulder, covered the remains of several pioneers.

The station was prettily laid out, the walks through the open space in front forming a large Union Jack. The houses were still of the usual primitive wattleand daub, but bricks and stones were being prepared for the permanent buildings.

The problem of the various languages required for intercourse with the natives was being seriously tackled. In Chinyanja, the common words of everyday life were already known, but notebooks were in constant requisition by all of us for new words or phrases and turns of language.

On my first Sunday service was held with the villagers and the children on the station. In the afternoon I accompanied a couple of missionaries and native rowers to a village six or eight miles to the South West. As the road journey by land was impracticable, by reason of hills and cliff,we went by boat, disturbing several ugly-looking hippopotami, which were uncomfortably curious. We also kept careful watch that we were not molested by the braves of the village, some of whom were not too friendly on account of slaves running off to the white man. No rifles or revolvers were carried by the missionaries, as they sought to establish their influence by moral rather than physical force. Runaway slaves were not infrequently received, but the masters were allowed to come in safely and state their case. When it was made out to a reasonable extent, the slaves if they wished to remain, were given work, with the proceeds of which they could buy their freedom, at an agreed rate.

The coast Arabs, many of whom stayed with Mponda, Jumbe and the others, knew well the practise of British men-of-war on the Zanzibar coast, who routinely would hunt down dhows and liberate the slaves. Not unnaturally they were hostile to any similar disturbance of their cruel trade on the Lake. The mission policy of not actively participating in anti-slavery action, but proceeding by way of education, remonstrance and reasoning proved itself in the end to be sound. Not infrequently big Arab chiefs, under the influence of drink, or on the arrival of their coast-caravans with powder and guns, threatened the white men. Often there were times of great anxiety, and war parties started, but they never reached the station. By negotiation, peace was again restored. This was of the highest importance in the case of Mponda. For our only means of communication with the coast was by the Shire River, down which the steamer would have to pass close to the high banks on which his villages were situated and from which volleys could have raked the little vessel from point-blank range.

Up in the hills to the west of the Lake were the warlike Angoni, descendants of the Zulus from the far south. They had once been unsuccessful in a raid entrusted to them by the great Chaka, and fearing the punishment they would receive if they returned to their chief, they had trekked northward. Crossing the Zambesi, they installed themselves in various groups in the highlands to the west of the Lake, where their Zulu war tactics made them invincible against the less warlike native tribes. Every year their bands went out north, south, east and west, capturing slaves, caffle, and crops, and 'washing the spears" of the young warriors in blood.

Dr. Laws, anxious to start a Mission among the Atonga natives near Bandawe, halfway up the western shore of the Lake, found them terrorized by the Angoni. Their villages were built for protection in the water (true lacustrine villages), and in stockades amid swamps or in other inaccessible places. To establish a station and save the natives, some arrangement must be made with the Angoni, and Dr. Laws decided to visit their principal chief, Mombera. James Stewart, cousin of Dr. James Stewart of Lovedale, an Indian Civil Service engineer., who while on furlough from India had given much assistance to the Mission, was to accompany him; and to represent the commercial side of civilization I was glad to join the expedition.

The first and obvious difficulty was to secure the necessary porters from among the Atonga to approach and enter the country of these bloodthirsty Angoni. Europeans, when travelling far from headquarters, require a considerable following to move their impedimenta. Not only are men required to carry tents, beds, cooking utensils, changes of clothes and food, but in a land where money is unknown, and where barter is the medium of exchange, one's purse is very bulky. Trusses of grey calico and of prints, bales of blankets, coils of brass wire and boxes of beads, may for a short expedition require the services of a dozen extra porters.

In this case hardly a man would accompany either the missionaries or myself. By this time the Mission had an outpost on the hills to the west at Kaningina, near the no-man's-land which lay between the Angoni and Atonga. This eased our difficulty. With the valuable assistance of a Lovedale native christian and William Koyi, whose native language was understood by the Angoni chiefs, communication had already been established withthe nearest villages in Angoniland, and Chipatula, an Angoni village headman, had paid a friendly visit to Kaningina. After exceptional trouble and palaver, the Atonga carried our loads to Kaningina, and Chipatula's men carried them into the borders of Angoniland. Thence with further trouble and delays, increasing as we approached the chief town, we got our loads carried short distances, sometimes only from village to village.

We were a party of three whites. With us were William Koyi, our Angoni interpreter and adviser as to Angoni customs, and our personal native servants and three or four mission boys who were willing to share the danger of the expedition into the heart of the enemy's country. Our visit was to be one of friendship and goodwill, supplemented by an offer to trade and to exchange for their ivory some of the many things natives valued, and which so far they had been practically unable to obtain. The name of Dr. Laws, as healer of the sick and wounded, was a strong point in our favour.

We allowed the fame of guns and rifles to pass ahead of us from camp to camp. We deemed it well worthwhile to expend some revolver and cartridges to let subsidiary chiefs see the difference between our firearms, which seemed to fire continuously without reloading and the muzzle-loaders which were the only guns they knew. Our reception at the villages we passed was not hostile, but a good deal of tact was required in resisting demands for presents, which, if complied with, would have caused us to reach Mombera's empty-handed and very airily clad, as the natives greatly coveted our European attire. Moreover, as this was a pioneer journey, intended to berepeated from time to time, it was very important that indiscriminate begging should be discouraged. We paid fairly for food supplied and suitably acknowledged presents given to us.

At length we arrived within a mile of Mombera's kraal, and sent on messengers to intimate our presence and ask for an interview. It was an anxious time. Night fell, and still no messenger returned. We were camped in our tents, not far from villages whence, should the reply be unfavourable, we might speedily have been overwhelmed by hordes of fierce warriors. We three, along with our native servants, kept alternate watches throughout the night, and in the forenoon of the next day a messenger returned inviting us to proceed. We afterwards learned that our proposal had been keenly debated by the headmen. So even was the feeling for and against us that they agreed to administer the poison ordeal to decide whether we should be received or not. The mwavi bark had been duly procured, pounded and mixed, and with due ceremony had been administered, fortunately not to a human being, but to a hen, which had thrown up the poison and recovered. So we were invited to an interview with the chief that he might consider what we had to say. The fate of our expedition had thus trembled in the balance of a hen's digestion.

We were conducted into the village, and encamped not far from the chiefs quarters. Our presents having been prepared, we had our first interview. Dr. Laws, through Koyi, explained the object of the missionaries in coming, at God's command, to tell the Africans what He had revealed of His laws in the Bible, and their own desire to live in friendship with the Angoni. But if that was to be so, these war-raids on the Atonga must cease, and then the missionaries would be glad to establish a station among them also. For the Angoni anything interfering with their warraids, the source of their power and wealth, was very unwelcome. But Mombera and some of his chiefs (among them the older ones who had already fought their battles) desired to have these strange white men, with their wisdom, their courage, and their power, as their friends. The white man's wonderful goods, which could be procured by trade, were an attraction.

We were thankful for the reception thus far accorded us. When we were walking in the outskirts of the village, some chiefs desired to see our guns, of which they had heard so much. Taking my Winchester repeater, holding seventeen cartridges, I got one of them to stick his knobkerrie into the base of a great anthill. At about fifty yards I fired at the round four-inch knob on the head of the stick. As nothing seemed to have happened I fired again and split the knob.

Examining it, they found that the first shot also had gone clean through it. It made an enormous impression, to have such shots on their side in the case of war was, to them, eminently desirable, and doubtless contributed to their wish to have us as friends.

Next day Mombera had a review of his warriors to show his power and greatness. We were accorded positions of honour beside him on a big ant-heap at one end of the great cattle kraal. Over five hundred men, equipped with bullock-hide shields, throwing and stabbing spears, and gay with feathers and war paint, entered the kraal. They were in six or eight companies, well marshalled two deep. They marched or danced in step, and, approaching the chief, they saluted and made low obeisance. Thereafter, followed war dances by the leaders of the companies in which they danced, leapt, stabbed, defended, and contorted themselves until perspiring and exhausted they gave place to others.

Ranks of lithe maidens, scantily clad in bead aprons, with long white wands held upright, joined in the manoeuvres, adding grace to the scene. A combined charge by the host warriors, right up to our feet, was somewhat of an ordeal. The leading warriors, perspiring, leaping, with their eyes gleaming with the lust of battle, their big stabbing-spears poised aloft, and followed by the serried ranks of the companies, came so close, that it required an effort of will to preserve a smiling face and calm demeanour. Especially was this difficult as, at the time, we were not aware what decision had been come to as to our offers of friendship.

We eventually departed with mutual expressions of goodwill, and thereafter concerted raids by the tribe on the Atonga practically ceased.

Having thus visited Lake Nyasa at several points of call, making ftiends with the chiefs and people, and having made a beginning of trade in ivory with the Arabs, I returned toward the coast.

A Mission station was subsequently established among the Angoni. The Rev. Dr. Elmslie's fascinating book, 'Among the Wild Angoni'. recounts the dangers. the adventures, and the patience called for before the establishment of the first school was permitted and the almost incredible changes effected, until these fierce Angoni, met in Council, voluntarily invited the British Administration to take charge of the country, and became loyal members of the British Empire.

# CHAPTER V

### 'THE LADY NYASA' GOES UP-RIVER

It was about the middle of March 1879 when, the Zambesi having risen and flooded its banks and filled the Balambwanda Channel, the 'Lady Nyasa' started on her trip to the great river.

Large floating islands impeded her; once or twice they drove down on her and whirled her round, so that it was with difficulty she could be freed. The winding channel of the Balambwanda was found choked with sudd, but as the steamer drew only fifteen inches she was able to make her way across the flooded plain. At last, the obstructions overcome, the Zambesi lay before us. Owing to the flood it was miles wide and about twenty-five feet above normal level.

It was late in the afternoon after a day of strenuous toil and anxiety. Difficulties with firewood, much of what had been prepared having been carried off by the floods, with floating islands or with shallows or eddies, still called for resource and patience. Some rivets sprang in the light plating, necessitating much baling.

When it seemed that all difficulties had been surmounted another serious trouble occurred Steaming out of the comparatively slack water of the Balambwanda into the swift-flowing Zambesi, the prow was caught by the current, and the steamer was swung heavily on to the shallow water on the flooded bank of the Balambwanda. All hands worked hard for some time, but in vain, and the native crew, tired with hard work, deserted. New men were enlisted from a neighbouring village, and arrived in canoes. In these the cargo was transported to some ground above water, on which we erected a staging of planks, and at last we hauled our steamer clear into the Zambesi and reloaded.

It was necessary before proceeding up-country to give her a thorough overhaul. In view of anticipated difficulties and of the desirability of deciding how and where such repairs should in future be made in these unknown tidal waters, I accompanied my brother in the steamer to the mouths of the Zambesi. As the river was miles broad and full from bank to bank, the run down was simple and delightful.

The Zambesi has six or eight principal mouths. The largest are so blocked by heavy sandbars as to be useless as entrances for ocean steamers. The Kongoni mouth is reached by a channel branching off from the main river towards the south at a right angle. Presumably most of the sand brought down by the floods is carried past this channel and is deposited in the slack water on reaching the ocean, so forming impassable shallows at the mouths of the main streams.

Similarly the most northerly channel of the delta, the Chinde River, also branches off from the main stream at more than a right angle, and with less sand carried into it has more water on the bar than the others.

The Kongoni was the one we made for. It is the most southerly of the mouths, and at that time was the best known. Steering was difficult in the deep and winding wooded channel between the main Zambesi and the Kongoni rivers. But we reached the mouth in due time and anchored on one of the many lateral channels. Here we were sheltered from the ocean storms by a sandy island, Inhanguruwe (the Isle of Pigs), a mile or so wide and many miles long.

On the Kongoni proper was a solitary reed-house, a recent erection by the Dutch firm in Quilimane, where their sole agent, a German named Ludwig Deuss, was lying very ill with fever. We were able to help him with quinine and palatable food, which put him on his feet while our steamer repairs were completed. Later Deuss assisted in furthering German interests in East Africa.

Mangrove trees, tall and straight, were abundant, growing in the deep muddy ooze of the swamp. Suitable trees near the river were chosen to construct a scaffolding on to which the steamer could be floated at the top of high spring tides. The wood was found to be exceedingly hard, and, when cut, was so heavy as not to float even in the salt water of the estuary. By lashing the logs alongside the steamer, they were, after much trouble, eventually transported to our chosen repairing beach. Here we found the neighbouring grass to be the home of myriads of mosquitoes, exceptionally rapacious and bloodthirsty, both by day and night. At this spot we had to wait, practically marooned, fourteen days till next spring tide floated the repaired and repainted steamer off again. Fortunately, on the desolate island game was fairly plentiful and buck formed an agreeable addition to our larder.

One Sunday we two managers crossed the estuary in the little six-feet dinghy to visit and take some fresh buck meat to the German invalid. In the afternoon the sea-breeze freshened, and dark clouds portended a storm. Hurrying back, we had barely time to get near the other side when the squall burst, and the heavy surf broke into the boat and filled her. We dragged her on to a bare sandbank, emptied her, and turned her over to make some shelter from the gale. Then, after a while, we were able, with the assistance of our one native, to carry her over to a more sheltered creek, and after a hard pull we regained the southern bank in safety.

While I took over duties on the coast, the journey of the lady Nyasa up the Zambesi and Shire was carried out under the leadership of my brother, in what would, to many have been impossible conditions.

The exceptional flood had spread over the valley for miles, destroying many villages, as was evident from huts and roofs floating past us out to sea. It had also carried away the stores of firewood prepared for the steamer, so that those on board had to stop at forests or villages on high ground and buy or cut down trees for fuel. Seldom could good dry trees be procured, so that raising steam was difficult and progress slow, and the constant cutting and sawing was hard on the crew. It went fairly well till the Morambala Marsh was reached. The Shire wound its way with constant S-bends through this muddy morass, extending to hundreds of square miles. In these days, before the desiccation of the riversand lakes, even in the dry season the mud banks would scarcely bear a man's weight.

The flood had floated off quantities of sudd from the higher reaches and lagoons, which came down in floating islands. As the river was overflowing its mud banks, the current at the S-bends was often sluggish, and acres of dense masses of sudd collected and blocked the river, while the water flowed in its deep channel below the floating masses.

Some of the first blocks encountered were removed by putting out grapnels into the thick mass at carefully selected spots, and with full steam downstream starting an enormous island down the current. The steamer then drew into the side, while the huge obstruction passed down. But further on the obstructions became heavier and thicker and more difficult to move. A view from the masthead made it clear that many days would be needed to make a way through. But away to the west lay a sheet of open water, and if the steamer could only be hauled through the dense growth of ten-feet high bango reeds, growing on the submerged bank of the river, all might be well. Her bows were therefore hauled round in that direction. My brother, though afraid of poisonous water snakes, swam through the reeds with a line twenty yards out, and made fast to a large armful of reeds tied together. Then they lightened the steamer and put the crew, black and white, overboard to trample down the reeds in front of the paddle-boxes, and with full steam ahead, and two strong men at the winch hauling on the line, they worked her through, inch by inch, into clear water, and made for a spot where some fishermen had landed from two canoes. They had caught two sharks about five and six feet long, which were still alive. These had probably got sick in the fresh water, and unable to make their way through the reeds to the river, had fallen an easy prey. Their livers were bought as a tit-bit for the native crew after their hard work. One of the fishermen had been bitten by a watersnake, but his leg was cauterised and dressed. Next day the fishermen pointed out a comparatively easy passage into the river above the sudd.

Other native fishermen in light canoes were met on higher reaches, and they supplied fish and information as to channels. They also brought firewood from the higher land on the north.

On several occasions progress seemed impossible, but by leading an amphibious life, doggedly persevering, and taking advantage of any weak spot in the line of obstruction, they at length, after a hand-to-hand fight of four and a half days, reached the open river, happy once more to have solid banks on which it was possible to land in comfort. That which had so often seemed impossible had been achieved.

As the waters fell to a more normal level, the increased current in the main river channel cleared away many of the obstructions, and the steamer, some weeks later, was able to move more easily. But until the volume of water became permanently lower (when, however, other difficulties caused by shallow sandbars and rocks gave trouble) the Morambala Marsh at certain states of the river was a formidable obstruction to navigation.

On this, as on all our early journeys, special care was taken to win and conserve the friendship of the chiefs and people of the villages bordering the river. We preserved a judicious mean between "stand-offishness" and familiarity, encouraging them to sell fowls, vegetables, and rice at reasonable standard prices, and to prepare firewood and place it where the steamer could come alongside and load.

Steaming past the river Ruo (an affluent of the Shire River from the north-east) and through the Elephant Marsh, then frequented by large herds of elephant and buffalo, the country of the Makololo was reached. These chiefs were the personal followers of David Livingstone, who had brought them from the then almost unknown country near the Victoria Falls, in his great journey from the Atlantic to the Indian Ocean. He had left them on the Shire, with the express instructions to hold the country till the British came again. By their bravery and general conduct these men had gathered round them sections of the Manganja and Yao tribes, and were now important chiefs. They accorded to the Mission and to ourselves a warm welcome. When the first party of the Livingstonia Mission arrived in their steamer Ilala in 1876, Ramakukan, the acknowledged chief of the Makololo, supplied the men, and assisted in the dismantling of the steamer and its carriage past the Murchison Cataracts. Owing to the hilly and rocky nature of that route, this was an important and difficult achievement, as a single missing or damaged part of the steamer might have disorganised the whole a expedition.

On the arrival at his village of the 'Lady Nyasa', Chipatula, another important Makololo chief, sold us quantity of ivory, which he kept stored on a small island. As they paddled to it, John seated himself on the edge of the canoe, but the chief begged him either to stand or to squat on the bottom for fear of crocodiles, which at this section of the Shire are particularly dangerous. Women drawing water do so from a high bank, dipping a small gourd fastened to the end of a long bamboo into the stream and filling their large earthenware pots laid on the bank, perhaps ten feet distant from where they stand. Many villages have a strong stockade in the water round some creek wherein the inhabitants can bathe in safety.

Farther on, Katunga was reached, the head of the lower river navigation. Here we established an important transport station of the Company, which existed until navigation was rendered impossible owing to the shallowness of the river.

# CHAPTER VI

### WEIRD IVORY PALAVERS

As we had now passed over our route as far as Lake Nyasa and bad seen it in one season of the year, we were able to formulate plans for the best conduct of our business with the men at our disposal. There were five stages to be supervised:

1. From Quilimane to Marendinny, on the Kwakwa, about five days by boat and canoe.
2. Overland portage about three miles to Maruru on the Zambesi.
3. By steamer (*Lady Nyasa*) seven days, some-times prolonged to three weeks (or if the steamer were under repair, by boat and canoe three to six weeks), up the Zambesi and Shire Rivers to Katunga.
4. Twenty-five miles to Blantyre and thirty-five miles more to Matope on the Upper Shire, again by portage.
5. To the north of Nyasa by the only craft available, the little Mission screw steamer '*Ilala*'. In all, a month's journey, if fate were extra kind.

The first stage was perhaps the most difficult. For the Kwakwa route we at first hired or purchased open boats, which were paddled in deep water by eight to ten natives, usually clad in dirty calico or native bark cloth, the minimum required for decency. They were also supplied with ten to twelve foot bamboo or other poles, by which when they could reach bottom they punted the boat along.

In the early days the usual shelter for a passenger was a semicircular erection of bent branches covered with grass for seven or eight feet near the stern of the boat. This excluded the fiercest rays of the sun and much of any rain that might fall. Soon we arranged to have light wooden houses to replace the grass, with painted canvas fastened on the roofs. As the boats, to escape the heavy currents in the middle of the stream, swept along the thick reeds or floating grass, they raised myriads of mosquitoes. Mosquito curtains were thus necessary for comfort, both by day and night. The substitution of a square-topped, firm, clean, airy wooden house for a rounded moving grass-erection, made all the difference to health on the four or five days journey required for this section.

Boxes or trusses of calico were usually packed as evenly as possible in the stern of the boat. On this foundation a mattress was spread, and the passenger often spent a couple of days on this divan, until, tidal water passed, the oozy mud gave place to clean sand. Then it was simple and pleasant to slip out of the boat on a sandy bank for the cooking and eating of meals.

So long as there was enough water to float the boats, splendid progress was made with the long punting poles wielded in perfect time by the natives standing on the thwarts of the boat, accompanied not uncommonly by a weird chant, led by the steersman or the bowman and responded to in chorus by the crew. All too often both progress and chorus would be brought to a sudden stop by the boat grounding on a sandbar. If vigorous punting with the poles failed to move her, the crew jumped into the water and tugging and shoving usually managed to get her over. In the dry season the boats and canoes were often dragged long distances over the sand to the detriment of paint, keel, and bilges.

During our first season the water was good and the channel fairly clear, but often great masses of sudd, (floating vegetation growing on the surface of lagoons and other slack water) caused much difficulty. One of the chief offenders was the Pistia stratiotes, which has the appearance of a healthy small green cabbage. It floats erect on the surface of the water, having long free roots. This and other weeds are often driven by wind into dense floating islands, where plants and roots get so firmly jammed together that they will bear the weight of natives walking on them. Or they may be gently carried down by the current to the exit of the lagoon, where they accumulate till they almost block the passage.

When the river rises in the early part of the rainy season, hundreds of these islands are caught by the current and borne downstream. A sharp bend of the river, a large tree, or a peculiarly-shaped sandbar may cause an obstruction and stop a large island. Then, under certain conditions, island gets jammed upon island, until the whole river, for six or eight feet deep, is blocked for hundreds of yards, the water flowing beneath or through this great mass of chaotic vegetation. These obstructions often close up the passages for months until a heavy and sudden rise in the river lifts them clear of what started the block, and they then continue their course as dense islands down to tidal waters, and often out to sea.

Loaded river boats encountering these blocks could sometimes be dragged over them, the combined crews of two or three boats pressing down the vegetation with their feet at less tightly-jammed parts. But sometimes goods and passengers had to be landed and the boats hauled by main force past the obstruction.

Another of our problems was to obtain a supply of regular labour. Our Portuguese agents assured us that we would be unable to secure it without the customary payments in "kachasso" - a strong alcohol. If crews for boats or canoes were wanted the messenger calling them usually carried kachasso. If house servants, or outdoor workers, were required, a preliminary drink was essential, and the larger the proportion of kachasso promised as wages the easier was it to secure men. Just beyond the confines of a Portuguese town - say Quilimane - there were numerous huts or booths on the principal paths displaying bottles of spirits which were seductively pressed on passers-by. In the afternoons and evenings these places became a snare to wayfarers. Scenes of debauchery and quarrelling were of constant occurrence. The effect on the morals, and on the economic value of the natives, was plainly visible.

We determined that we would not countenance such practices, and at first therefore had much difficulty in securing necessary crews and workers. We paid them full rates of wages, but no liquor. If old topers wanted the latter they could barter some of their wages for drink. But gradually the situation improved, and, treating the natives fairly, we had ultimately no more difficulty than others in securing the men we required. Once beyond Portuguese influence the question was less difficult, as no payments were made in spirits, and they were seldom asked for. We proved that spirits were not necessary for procuring labour or foodstuffs even in Portuguese territory, and eventually succeeded in having the trade prohibited in Nyasaland.

How this was effected may be told here. At the Berlin Congress in 1884, when the European Powers met to discuss Congo developments and the future of Central Africa. A small party from Scotland, consisting of the Rev. Dr. Laws of the Livingstonia Mission, Mr. William Ewing, then Secretary of the African Lakes Company, and myself as one of the founders and managers, attended to watch over the interests of Nyasaland. We were able to lay telling facts before the British representative there, and also assure him that Nyasaland had been so far opened up on the principle of the exclusion of the liquor trade. In the best interests of the natives we pressed for regular restriction of the hurtful trade in Nyasaland and in other African territories so far commercially undeveloped. We were gratified that the Congress agreed, by International Treaty, to the exclusion for all time of the sale of spirits to natives in the territories of the Upper Zambesi basin, and far inland, beyond the Congo watershed.

The demoralising and degrading effects of the spirit trade are only too well known, and I attribute to this policy of prohibition a large part of British success in East Central Africa It has unquestionably proved of far-reaching effect in promoting the welfare of the native races there.

I look upon what we were thus able to achieve as one of the permanent advantages bestowed upon the country by the Africa Lakes Company.

Our first attempts to trade with the Arabs within the sphere of our operations were disappointing. They knew to a rupee the latest price of ivory at Zanzibar. For them slaves on the Lake were cheap and plentiful and could be sold at a profit, along with the ivory, on the coast. So the Arabs would not take less than Zanzibar prices when trading ivory with us. Further, they chiefly wanted guns and powder, while we only in exceptional circumstances would sell any weapons. Beyond an exchange of presents and a beginning of personal knowledge little resulted.

Later we secured fair quantities of ivory, but it was slow and laborious work. One was often not allowed to handle or weigh a tusk. We got over that by giving a little extra, after the sale was completed, because we found the tusk when weighed was a little heavier then we had guessed. Then they regularly pressed us to weigh the tusks, which was more satisfactory. We could then examine them for flaws or disease and make sure that none of the common native tricks of filling lead or clay into the hollows had been perpetrated; we also knew better what price could be afforded.

The work was not without interest and entertainment. Jumbe would trade his ivory only at night. Probably he did not want his natives to know how much the white man would give, and so spoil his purchasing market. Late at night we would row in from the steamer, keeping clear of hippos, and get carried ashore from the dinghy, and, accompanied by two or four natives with trade goods, would stumble along the dark native path to the veranda of his big house. After salutations and small talk-and here our knowledge of Kiswahili was valuable-we would approach the question of ivory. He would hardly admit there was any in the village, but at length his men would bring a tusk of moderate dimensions. Some impossible sum would be asked, this would be met by a low offer on our part. Then much talk, indignation, chaffing, and the tusk would be taken away and another brought, or possibly we commenced to pack up and go away. It was a weird scene. The dark veranda was lighted up dimly by a wood fire, or by a candle-lantern shielded with glass from assaults of moths, flying ants, and mosquitoes, so as to prevent the light being extinguished under a funeral pyre of burned bodies. The Arab, clad in white kansu, with a long gold-embroidered black robe and large turban, was seated cross-legged on a mat. The white trader sat cross-legged on another; or preferably (if the sitting was to last several hours) on the camp-chair he had brought with him, not only to save him from cramp, but also to give him a better elevation from which to lay down the law. Behind the Arab stood some of his trusted men or slaves with little of them visible but gleaming teeth and sparkling eyes.

The moan of the wind outside; farther off; the beat of the tom-tom; and in the distance the weird howl of the hyena, accentuated the eeriness of the situation. Who or what might be in that darkness that surrounded us as we sat in the light? What armed warriors stood close to us as we had stumbled up the narrow path? We knew not.

After 'good-bye' had been said, a more reasonable offer would be made. The price was coming near business. Something, a lamp, a shirt, a gaudy waistcoat, would be added to the trusses of white and coloured cloths, and at length one tusk was bought. If no caravan had left recently for the coast, and there was much ivory in the village, sometimes eight or ten tusks would thus be bought. By ten o'clock, or sometimes very much later, the adieus were said, and the strange procession marched down to the boat.

# CHAPTER VII

### ESTABLISHING HEADQUARTERS

For headquarters we selected a site in the Shire Highlands (twenty-five miles from Katunga, and one mile distant from Blantyre, the central station of the Church of Scotland Mission), and called it 'Mandala". This was my brother's native name, denoting the reflection of light from his spectacles.[1] Although at first only referring to headquarters, this name was gradually applied to all the Company's stations throughout Nyasaland and Rhodesia, and is still recognised by the natives as synonymous with fair dealing and good treatment.

For some time after our arrival we had the hospitality of one of the small houses of the Blantyre Mission. A block of well-timbered land, 7000 acres in extent, separated from Blantyre by the Mudi stream, was purchased from Kapeni of Soche, and the first brick building in Nyasaland was erected upon it. It was 124 feet long by 30 feet broad. The Blantyre end, which had a spacious veranda in front, was used as the dwelling house, and the remainder was utilised for bulk and transit stores.

Experiments were made with different clays to find that best adapted for the manufacture of bricks. To obviate cracking during the process of drying, chopped dry grass was at first added after the manner of the ancient Egyptians. We had no bricklayers, and to minimise the labour falling on the senior manager we made especially large, heavy, sun-dried bricks, 18 x 8 square inches. The clay was thoroughly tramped by natives feet and rammed into a mould made of boards, and dried slowly in the shade; the bricks became very hard and strong. As we had relays of natives carrying these to the wellhead, great progress was made. When the natives became expert with level and plummet, and able, under supervision, to build a well-bound wall, we adopted the usual nine-inch brick as more easily fired and quickly handled.

Poles and young trees in these days were plentiful and long. The natives soon became expert thatchers, and the original Mandala store, if somewhat dark on account of veranda roofs, was erected strong, cool, and spacious.

Many a wayfarer passing on to the Lake was glad to place his camp-bed in the big living room, where he could be safe from lions and hyenas which prowled about the precincts. To keep these animals and any would-be thieves at a distance from the cattle and stores, we erected a stockade of native trees (many of which took root), backed by a thick hedge of thorns. Two heavy wooden doors, hanging on overhead wheels, barred the main road through the stockade leading from Katunga, on the lower Shire, to Blantyre and the north. For many years armed watchmen guarded the gates and verandas, but they were themselves sometimes the watched, as on more than one occasion hyenas seized them while sleeping and attempted to drag them off.

One day a hippopotamus marched through the garden. As there was no deep water within fifteen miles, where he came from and what he wanted was a mystery.

Lining the stockade was a long row of guava trees, one of the first of our importations to bear fruit. Oranges, limes, pineapples, Cape gooseberries, and European vegetables later formed a valuable addition to the commissariat. Mandala House, a large two-storied building, was erected in 1882 as a home for the resident manager and general office. Not only had it dining and drawing-rooms, but several guest chambers, where practically all passers-by in the early days received hospitality.

This house, with its upper storey, for long was to the native one of the wonders of the countryside, and they came long distances to see one house on the top of the other. The staircase was most alarming, and a fearless native, who would cross a deep, swift-flowing river on a fallen tree, would creep laboriously and tremblingly up the broad easy stairs on his hands and knees.

These were the times of hostile raids. The Yaos and Angoni were still sources of dread. It was therefore important for the protection of the Europeans and goods that we should have a defensible station of considerable size.

Some years later supplementary iron doors and shutters were provided for the lower storey of Mandala House. A new store was built of burned brick 150 feet to the rear. It was 100 feet long, solid brick to the outside, and was flanked by two protruding towers which, loop-holed on the second storey, commanded the front and sides. These sides, also twelve feet high, backed by stores and outhouses, came in a direct line from the store towers to the walls of Mandala House, thus rendering the sides defensible both from the top veranda of the house and from the towers of the store. A large arched door, for carts and carriers, also guarded by an iron gate, led through the centre of the store into the court. There was thus provided not only large stores and a dwelling-house for the safeguarding of the Company's property and staff, but a large enclosed compound where our villagers could take refuge in times of danger.

Our principal native workers and hunters were allowed to settle on Mandala Estate, and villages sprang up. No rent was charged, but the natives were available when required for the transport of goods and passengers at the usual full rates of pay.

At first it was difficult to induce the natives to undertake work of any kind. It was only after they had learned to trust the white man that they would accept weekly payments, in calico or other goods, for their work. As their confidence increased, they preferred to work for a month and receive their payments in larger pieces of calico or print. Indeed, they soon became so trustful that, when the steamer was delayed by disturbances on the river, they cheerfully accepted for work or goods, little chits of paper bearing an initial and a given number of yards, to be honoured on the arrival of supplies from the coast. On the occasion of a Portuguese expedition against the Makololo, they continued working for over six months, quite satisfied that our scraps of paper would be honoured after arrival of supplies. This system of currency continued until the introduction of coins. Eggs and small baskets of flour were usually bartered for beads and needles; fowls and services rendered were generally paid for by unbleached or coloured calico.

In process of time the Company was recognised by the natives as a potent influence in the land, and they brought all sorts of disputes for decision. Natives are inclined to be litigious, and "mirandu" or palavers were very common. The commonest sources of trouble were runaway wives and decamp-mg slaves. Issues between chiefs, cases of theft, and the outcome of drunken brawls were often submitted to us for adjudication. Even runaway wives generally accepted the decision to return to their husbands, usually with some provision that their treatment should be bettered. Many slaves were allowed to work for their freedom at an agreed price. Domestic slavery was such a universal institution throughout Central Africa that it had at first to be recognised and ameliorated rather than abolished or ignored. We sought, therefore, in these early days to treat cases brought before us on broad humanitarian grounds. It was our invariable habit fully to hear what both sides had to say, and it was remarkable that a judgement given in good faith was usually accepted by both sides. The disputants said: "The white man has considered the case and we will abide by his decision." This was done even in instances where perhaps long afterwards we found a mistake, founded upon wrong evidence, had been made.

In one instance the carrying out of a judgement closely affected our household. Chuanganya, the girl-wife of an old Yao, came complaining that she had been very cruelly treated. At the 'mirandu' the husband could not deny the charge, and had to admit that in beating her he had broken her tooth. The Mosaic Law on the subject was read in their language, and with the approval of those present the girl was declared free. The only stipulation was that she should not marry again till the old man was repaid her dowry, and until that happened she should remain in the care of a white donna. She was brought to our veranda and interviewed by my wife, who was rather averse to taking a woman into the house. But when she saw the forlorn, wretched look of the girl, she agreed to befriend her, and Chuanganya turned out a real treasure. In order to give her something to do, Mrs. Moir brought a native brush with a bamboo so that she might sweep the steps. When she saw this she thought she was going to be beaten and threw herself on the ground and grovelled for mercy.

It did not take long to make a complete change in her condition, both physical and mental. Well washed and oiled, clad in native costume, her face beaming with contentment and good nature, she worked in the house, and by and by accompanied Mrs. Moir on a long journey to Tanganyika and back. All the other servants resident about the establishment being "boys," older and younger, Chuanganya slept alone in a storeroom. Once when I was from home she resolved to protect her mistress, and coming to her room she crept bodily under the large carpet and, despite the lack of ventilation, slept soundly

Suitors turned up in course of time, but her ladyship, as servant and companion of the donna, knew she was well off and was fastidious in her tastes. One day when I was at a distance from the house a man approached me on the subject, so I scribbled on a scrap of paper: "This is a suitor for Chuanganya: will she have him?" He reached the house with the document carefully carried in a cleft twig and handed it to Mrs. Moir. She asked Chuanganya if she knew the man, but she disclaimed acquaintanceship. When told that he wanted her for his wife she looked him over and, with a toss of her head, declared that she would not marry a man with one eye.

She remained with us till we left for home. We were glad to learn shortly afterwards that an eligible suitor had turned up and that she is now happily married.

---

Notes:

1. The native name of Mandala, given to John Moir, is still used as the trading name for The Africa Lakes Corporation. n fact in 1977 the African Lakes Corporation became Mandala Limited.

All trading stations run by African Lakes in the 1920's and 1930's were prefixed by Mandala. As an example my grandfather Robert Carr Thomson, who worked as a storeman then general merchant for the company, was based at Mandal Karonga, Mandal Blantyre and Mandala Dedza at various times of his career.

For Frederick Moir, he was blessed with the native name of "Chindevu" which meant 'Great Beard', not surprisingly when you see the photograph of the author on the jacjet of this book.

# CHAPTER VIII

### A POISON ORDEAL ON A ROYAL SCALE

Trial by ordeal is practised by many kinds of primitive peoples. The common form among East Africans in our time was mwavi, bark poison. If a man or woman were accused of any crime or misdemeanour, protestations of innocence were usually accompanied by an offer to drink mwavi. Among natives near our stations it was often resorted to, usually at night, lest the white man should interfere and insist on investigations and a proper trial, with examination of witnesses.

Some years after my first visit to Mombera, I was an involuntary spectator of a wholesale administration of the poison ordeal at the village of Chikusi. The chief of another branch of the Angoni tribe, some fifty miles south of Lake Nyasa, had been raiding as far east as the Shire and even across it. I therefore determined to go up and visit the chief with offers of trade and peace.

When about fifteen miles from his village we had great difficulty in securing guides and porters. We hoped to get Palali, a big chief, to accompany us, but while he was friendly he would not appear. We appreciated his reluctance when we learned that in the previous year Nyamuka, a neighbouring friendly chief, who had introduced strangers and had given them a small tusk in return for presents, had been called up by Chikusi, on the pretext of having tried to procure medicine from the strangers, to bewitch him. He had to drink mwavi and died. Palali had also to undergo the ordeal, but recovered.

We sent on two village chiefs to announce our arrival. They returned to say there was mourning at headquarters that day, but we might come on the next. That evening we heard terrible stories of Chikusi's cruelty. He was specially hard on chiefs with the characteristic Zulu ring head dress, probably because he deemed them possible rivals for the chieftainship. Only the previous morning five such had been summoned by Chikusi and killed; the death drums were still beating.

Next day our guide took us within a mile of the village, pointed it out, and then decamped. We pitched our tents and waited. On the morrow five elderly headmen came to interview us and learn our business. We were invited to camp nearer the village, and many palavers ensued.

On the afternoon of the second day a general helter-skelter of onlookers attracted our attention to the approach of a very portly dame, the king's mother, while from another set of houses emerged a very fat man, the chief. He squatted down about thirty yards from my tent, the royal lady came a little nearer. Every one in sight, ourselves excepted, was now squatting in a most reverential manner. After a moment or two I sent one of my men to invite the king to my tent. This invitation Susi conveyed to the principal of half a dozen councillors, sitting twenty yards behind him. The latter crept forward to Chikusi, and, kneeling, whispered the invitation. In a moment he returned and by a movement of the lips signified the king had assented. But royalty must not hasten, so the chief sat another five minutes in solitary dignity.

Then the queen-mother made a move towards us, and with five attendants pretty well filled the tent. Shortly after, his majesty entered, and was seated. No portable chair or couch would have stood his enormous weight, and we had prepared a special seat by rolling a hair mattress in a thick waterproof cover. From his appearance, and the age of his mother and his children, I guessed him to be about thirty three years old. He was clad in a common blue calico sheet. While he watched some of the white man's curious ways, I got a snapshot photo of him, which showed his enormous size. By promising to get a shirt made for him I obtained his net waist measurement, which was fifty-five inches.

Long palavers followed, and my presents were sent on next day. Friendship towards the whites was promised, no raids to be allowed east of the Upper Shire River, and he would be glad to see us back. There was much delay before he sent down a small tusk as a return present, and several days more were spent endeavouring to begin a trade in ivory.

It was during this period that the mwavi drinking took place. An order had been sent round the country summoning all the chiefs wives from the various villages and a large number of villagers to come to prove their innocence of irregularities. Within sight of our tents a booth was erected for Chikusi and his headmen: thousands of natives gathered in the open plain to witness the proceedings.

We recognised the medicine man as one who had been sitting near our tent the day before. Now he was arrayed in an enormous headgear of feathers, standing out fully twelve inches from his head and down to his waist behind. Round his shoulders he wore a long cape of tails of skin and fur. He had on a loin-cloth and the usual bracelets and ornaments of a headman, and two attendants carried bags made of goat-skins. Near him sat the king's mother and about forty of the chiefs wives. A little later Chikusi arrived with twenty followers. Seeing us in the distance he sent for some sweets, for which he and his mother had developed a great partiality.

Six of the wives approached the medicine man and sat down. Chikusi was then asked by him if these women were to take the ordeal, and he referred them to his mother. She asked the women if they wanted to drink, and they all replied "Yes." Had they refused they would doubtless have been speared on the spot as confessedly guilty. The next step was to ask the king to give cloth that the medicine bags might be opened. He gave two yards. The bags were accordingly opened, and several pieces of bark three or four inches square were chosen by the pounder, and put into an ordinary wooden mortar.

The women, two old and four young, were accused of having taken goods belonging to the chief, and also of adultery. Chikusi was asked if they would have to drink twice on the separate counts, but intimated that once was enough. All the time he was laughing and joking with his men. Some of the women who had fasted since the previous day were greatly agitated, and one was laughing so hysterically that water was brought and given to her

The pounder then pounded the bark for several minutes, adding a handful of water, and resumed pounding. He did this half a dozen times. Then the principal medicine man began to address the mwavi. In his hand he held a neat thin stick two feet long, surmounted by a small ball, and with this he gesticulated and struck the mortar.

"If the women have taken their master's goods," he cried, "let the mwavi kill; if not, let them go home to their villages." The words were repeated in regard to the second offence of infidelity. In his invocations he pranced about between the women and the mortar and worked himself into a frenzy.

Adjuring the mwavi again to do its work, he fell back, and his assistants, taking a couple of drinking gourds that might hold half a pint, plunged them into the mixture and gave them to the women as they came up two by two. As the woman who had been so frightened took the stuff she called out to another in the crowd. "If I die, take the baskets of goods in my hut and give them to the chief" He callously responded, "Let her die. I will not take the goods, they belong to the medicine man."

Some drank eagerly, others falteringly, but drink they must. When all had partaken they were guided to a place in the plain where they were allowed to lie down and rest or wander about. Two of the six women died, their bodies were left exposed and parties of young men armed with spears and clubs immediately dashed off to kill their relatives and seize their property. That night the plain resounded with the yells of hyenas as they fought over the corpses.

Contrary to my expectation, the hysterical woman, who willed her property to the chief, recovered. I saw her later, a goat had been killed to celebrate her innocence. So far as I could judge, the mixture on this occasion was doled out impartially. If fear or excitement tended towards absorption of the poison and consequent death, this woman should have died. But these mwavi drinkings were doubtless attended by much knavery. If any man accumulated cattle or goods, those who envied him or feared him (often his chief) would get up a charge of witchcraft against him and his family. If any died, the relatives would be killed the property annexed, while none would dare to cast doubt on the ordeal.

Another day intervened, and in deference to our expostulations no drinking took place. Late at night some women, returning home after feeding the mwavi drinkers, passed my tent. On my expressing sympathy, their pent-up feelings broke forth. In hurried whispers, watching to see there were no eavesdroppers, they inveighed against the frequency of these orgies and the regime under which they were possible. Yes, they had drunk mwavi, but had vomited. This was said with pride, and showed their belief in the ordeal. Of course, if an innocent man drank and recovered, the mwavi "told true," and he believed in it all the more. If an innocent man died, all believed him guilty; and, being dead, he could not contradict the allegation.

Two days after the last ordeal I saw twenty-nine women, wives of the chief, and twenty-three young men, his followers, being marshalled to the drinking-place. After them about seventy more wives, and later a single man. In the afternoon the plain was covered with groups of those who had drunk and their sympathisers. It was a horrible spectacle. One young man died early, and another seemed too far gone. The latter had been sent by the chief the previous day to sell us a tusk.. We encouraged him to try and walk about, and were told later that he recovered.

We heard that there was to be a drinking on a larger scale still, and refusing to remain, we left Chikusi, protesting against his cruel customs. He listened quietly, but would not delay the drinking, though he promised to keep his bargain about not raiding our neighbours; and, so far as I remember, he kept his word. Shortly afterwards a branch of the Livingstonia Mission was opened in his country.

As we struck our tent, we saw the plain hill of new victims, they came down in long lines. We estimated that there were two hundred in sight, and more were to come later on. It was with a feeling of deep thankfulness and relief that I and my little party of half a dozen men and carriers left the scene of these horrible proceedings which we had been powerless to prevent.

# CHAPTER IX

### CUTTING THE SLAVE-ROUTES

In combating the slave trade by developing commerce, it was important to cut its routes far inland. For some hundreds of miles from the Zanzibar coast, the population was comparatively sparse, the baneful trade having done its work. The slavers had since gone farther afield. The populous regions to the west of Nyasa and Tanganyika were a favourite source of supply for both slaves and ivory, a providential combination in the eyes of the Arabs. The Company's idea, therefore, was to obstruct their routes by placing steamers on the rivers and lakes, and by offering fair prices and transporting the stuff by water to obviate the necessity for raiding and slave-carrying.

To cut one of the chief routes, however, Nyasa and Tanganyika must be joined, hence urgent instructions were sent out that one of us should explore the country between the lakes and proceed as far as Pambete at the south end of Lake Tanganyika. This was over two hundred miles north-west of Nyasa, and the intervening plateau was mountainous and unexplored, with no known direct route. My brother was selected for the task.

Of the other four Europeans on the staff, two were required on the steamer, as it took some years before the natives could be trusted to undertake any serious work about the engine and boiler. With the deterioration of the steel hull-plates, repairs and patching were a constant source of delay and vexation. That left one manager and one tradesman to superintend the forwarding and dispatch of goods and mails, the checking of deliveries and shortages, the initiation of trading, the building of stations and store and the bookkeeping of the Company. As the staff had their share of tropical fevers, etc., one wonders, on looking back, how the business was carried on. It meant working far into the night at correspondence and book-keeping. One or two men arrived to replace withdrawals, but it was not until my brother went home in 1882 that an increased staff, sufficient to occupy the more strategic points, was engaged and sent out.

On reaching Lake Nyasa, John visited Mombera, the Angoni chief, re-establishing our relations, and securing some trade. Marching farther west for about a week, he reached Kambombo, a populous centre, through which Livingstone had passed on his way westward in 1870. Thence he proceeded two days march farther north to Tembwe's, and returned to Bandawe.

In these and in all our various journeys in unknown and uncharted country, we mapped out our routes and locations as a small contribution to geographical science. By observing two stars with sextant and artificial horizon we were able to get our position of latitude north or south to within a hundred or two yards. The longitude was usually calculated by compass bearings from known hill and at times by an occultation of Jupiter's moons, or by lunar observations. At Bandawe John met Mr. James Stewart, C.E., and with him planned the expedition to Tanganyika. This was in 1879. Joseph Thomson, the well-known African traveller, had just reached the north end of Lake Nyasa overland from the Zanzibar coast and passed on towards Tanganyika, leaving letters reporting his progress. They planned to overtake him, but my brother, having developed a malarial abscess on his foot, had to abandon the expedition at Mwiniwanda, and Mr. Stewart proceeded alone, overtaking Mr. Thomson at Tanganyika.

In November of the same year, John recovered from the abscess and passed down the Songwe valley to the country of the Wamambwe or Wankonde. He visited Mwakusa and Manjawara, and bought from the latter a few acres of ground on the Lake shore at the north bank of the Mbashi River. Here he arranged with the chief to build a house for the Company.

With Mwakusa as guide, he shot several elephants. In the hope of catching a young one, he prepared ropes from buffalo hide. A cow elephant with a youngster had been shot, they tried to secure the calf. The villagers, keen for "nyama" (meat), assembled in great force, and surrounded the calf at a safe distance while John and his boys sought to lasso him. He was about the size of a native cow and remarkably agile and bellicose. Twice one or more of his legs were in the nooses, but he managed to escape. Over and over again they caught his tail, and were whisked along at express speed when he suddenly stopped and turned sending them flying and then the elephant charged one of the would-be captors. Noticing that he always charged a single individual, and hoping to keep him in the vicinity of the nooses, John stood his charge but slipped and was knocked down. The elephant got its trunk round his neck, and his little 3-inch tusks into his back, whereupon two of the natives immediately shot it, to the grief, but also the relief, of my brother who had one or more ribs broken. In due time he recovered and returned to Mandala.

From the information gained by Mr. Stewart, Mr. James Stevenson, our Chairman, was so convinced that a road could be made to complete the African Lakes route from the coast to Tanganyika that early in 1881 he offered to subscribe £4000 to carry out this project on which he had set his heart. Mr. Stewart, whose Indian experience was a great asset, was appointed road engineer, and with an assistant work was begun.

The first ten or twelve miles on the plain, including the crossing of the Rukuru River at the best ford, presented no great engineering difficulty. But natives had to be enlisted and trained to work for more than a day or so at a time. They had also to be taught to live at peace with villagers from other places, and to use suitable tools. The difficulties inherent in starting a new work in a savage land had to be overcome by patience, tact, and firmness.

Outdoor work on the dry, treeless plain is very trying during the heat of the day, mosquitoes, moths, and flying ants are very annoying at night, while scorpions or snakes have also to be guarded against. There were many lions and hyenas, but in these early days, before the rinderpest[1] destroyed the major part of the buffaloes and buck, they were not aggressive.

Natives, through whose gardens the road was led, or who considered they had grievances against the native workers, added considerably to the work and worry falling on Mr. Stewart, in addition to the actual difficulties of road-making. Fevers and tropical sickness were present as usual.

A heavy hill up and down was avoided by cutting a road along the side of a steep pass above the river. Another valley was crossed, and then the ascent to the great inland tableland began up the Ferauri Hill. The next fifty miles were very difficult, being steep and also so far from water as to admit work being done only during, or soon after, the rainy season. The steepest ascents were overcome by zigzags cut in the hillside, while rocks and boulders were removed to secure a good passage. When work was impracticable on the first hill section, it was recommenced on the plateau beyond Mwiniwandas and on to Soki.

Prospecting over these difficult hills to select the best contours was heavy work. Supervising the turning up of soil in the swamps and valleys was specially trying. Greatly to the grief of all, Mr. Stewart succumbed to fever and dysentery when only short sections of the hill work had been finished. Volunteers being called for, William McEwan, a gifted young engineer, undertook the charge and accomplished further long sections. He also gave his life in the heroic endeavour to open this line of between Nyasa and Tanganyika.

The road from lake to lake was not completed till many years later, when the British South Africa Company, having assumed the reins of government, filled in the gaps in the first section and carried a road available for wagons right through to Tanganyika. In recognition of the initiative, perseverance, and liberality of its founder, the road is still officially called the Stevenson Road.

As a fitting memorial of the many altruistic labours performed by James Stevenson, there stands in Central Africa, near Karonga, on the road which bears his name, an

Ionic cross in Kondowe stone, erected by our Corporation.

Notes:

1. Rinderpest was and is a virulent virus affecting cattle and cloven footed animals. Similar to foot and mouth disease, but much more deadly. Eradicated in Europe around 1877 it still occurs in Africa and Asia where it can kill 9 out of every 10 animals it infects.

# CHAPTER X

### ROUTED BY A HIPPO

The ordinary business of life was sometimes varied by adventure. On one occasion Mr. James Stewart, C.E., and I left Mandala to proceed to Lake Nyasa. The mission steamer 'Ilala' was having her boiler repaired at Matope, our transport station on the Upper Shire. We arrived a day before she was ready to sail and fortuitously we had with us a new teak dinghy to replace the original one which was worn out.

So to utilise our spare day we decided to explore the river down towards the cataracts to ascertain if there might be a good landing nearer Blantyre, and so reduce the thirty-five miles portage to Matope. The little dinghy comfortably held four, so we took two natives to row. We had two rifles, a shot gun, cooking gear for the day, and a new camera to photograph the falls and any suitable landing place.

We found this part of the Shire, undisturbed by the passing steamer, to be the haunt of many hippopotami. The broad, deep river made many curves. The current ran most swiftly along the outer banks of the bends, while on the opposite bank it was slack and sometimes formed a backwater. In practically every inner bend there were one or two hippos and sometimes eight or ten. It was simple to keep in the swift current while running with the stream, and any aggressive beast was warned off with a shot. A mile or two down we espied, standing on the right bank, a buffalo, which, if secured, would be a valuable addition to the larder for ourselves and the native workers. Drifting down noiselessly with the current we fired simultaneously. Our quarry fell in his tracks. To preserve the meat from hyenas and vultures it was necessary to cut the animal up, hang the quarters on trees, and cover up all traces. The boys having omitted to bring any knives, had to make do with my pocket-knife, a rather prolonged proceeding. Eventually the meat was safely stowed away, and we proceeded, carrying with us a few tit-bits for lunch.

We reached the first rapids without finding any suitable landing-place and after photographing the falls had lunch and proceeded on our return journey. This was a slower process, as we were not able to use the slack water on account of the hippos. We kept nearly mid-stream, out of the swiftest current, and at a considerable distance from the animals.

All went well till we reached our buffalo. We landed and stowed a hind leg below the thwarts, and took also a supply of the tenderer parts for the use of our mess. The boat was now overloaded, making rowing more difficult, but the natives were anxious to carry as much as possible for their companions. We had not proceeded many hundred yards when a hippo bull, lord of a numerous herd in a slackwater, nearly one hundred yards away, gave a menacing bellow, raised his head and shoulders clear from the water, and plunged in our direction.

Seeing he meant mischief, Mr. Stewart and I turned our rifles in his direction, at full cock, ready to give him a hot reception when he next rose to get his bearings and attack us.

We waited in suspense but he did not appear, and we had just remarked that he seemed to have thought better of it when, without warning, his teeth crunched through the bottom of the boat. In the same movement he pulled the keel with such a wrench towards himself, that I, sitting on the seat just above him, was heaved right up into the air clear of the opposite seat and was plunged into the water on the landward side. I went down feet first and when I came to the surface I saw my new helmet floating away.

I still held my .500-express rifle and regretted that filled with water it could not be used against the hippo. Then I considered whether I should try and carry it ashore. But we were thirty to forty yards from the bank in a crocodile infested river with a swift current. I had on a thick tacketed marching boots. Outside my coat was a strong leather belt with a heavy .350 Webley revolver and a pouch with express and elephant cartridges. The whole rig-out was far from conducive to swimming.

Taking mental note of my approximate position, I dropped the express rifle and made for the shore, keeping carefully at right angles to the current, not against it. Being a strong swimmer and at home in and under water, I made good progress.

At the first charge of the hippo, the two natives, wearing only light loin-cloths, plunged into the water and reached the shore first. Mr Stewart, anxious if possible to save the boat if the hippo would leave it, remained in it for a minute or two. When he saw the hippo's teeth again crunching the bottom, he realised it would be unsalvable. Throwing off his coat and belt he slipped into the water and followed me.

When still fifteen or twenty yards from the shore I was nearly played out. Overweighted as I was with sodden clothes and equip[ment, I turned to swim on my back, but almost immediately went under. Stewart, now close behind me, took my hand and guided me, swimming under water for the last few yards till we reached the bank. Our natives weer at hand to receive us and with their assistance we pulled ourselves beyond the immediate danger of crocodiles. I was full of water but, lying on my face with head very low, I soon got rid of the most of it, though I was left with a racking headache. I improvised new headgear out of a handkerchief, leaves and grass. On pushing through the thicket we discovered that we had not reached land but that deep water was all around. We had no desire to swim again that day, especially in slack waters, where crocs were likely to lurk.

At one place, where, though the water was quite deep, a belt of papyrus and other plants grew between our island sandbank and the shore, we determined to attempt a crossing.

The two natives led and bent armfuls of papyrus towards each other, and tramping over this not much more than waist deep we reached dry land.

Progress up the bank of the river was impossible, owing to the bango reeds, often fifteen to twenty feet long, and the prairie grass six or seven feet high. Game paths from the forest to the river were comparatively frequent and open, (so long as no hippos were feeding inland, which, if disturbed would rush with irresistible force to the water) we could easily reach the forest.

Passing a great solitary tree, we found it inhabited by a flock of guinea-fowl. Mr Stewart, who (with his own revolver at the bottom of the river) was a dead shot, tried three shots with mine, but failed to bag one. In our position we dared not use more cartridges.

Reaching the forest, where the undergrowth was comparatively scanty, we marched a couple of miles upstream and then judged it prudent to reach the river bank again to ascertain if we were opposite Matope. No sooner had we entered the long grass of the plain, than the thunder of the hoofs of a large herd of buffalo warned us of danger ahead. As we had only one revolver in the party that path was barred. Continuing our march, we came on a more open plain which must have been a favourite feeding-ground of game and hippo, as the grass was short. A considerable distance off was the river, to which we thankfully made our way. But one more obstacle intervened. It was a deep depression, about twenty feet broad, full of water. We had to wade this, chest deep, before reaching the banks of the Shire River.

Our first aim was to ascertain where we were, and to communicate with our friends. We could see some distance upriver, but downstream was damp ground with high reeds, and a bend limiting our view. We were alone in the bush. In vain we tried to find or break a path through the reeds. It became so dark that we could not see the loin cloth of the native walking immediately in front, So we returned to the open bank of the river to camp for the night.

The sun had set and the swift, tropical darkness was on us. Our clothes were again nearly dry, but our matches were totally destroyed. With a gun-flint I had in my pocket, and my knife, we spent some time each in turn trying to light some unsuitable tinder. As lions were numerous, fire was indispensable. I at last procured it by opening a cartridge and rubbing gunpowder into a bit of a native's loin-cloth. On firing a pistol shot we set the cloth alight.

We did not need to tell our boys to be carefully, they nursed the little flame as if their lives depended on it, and we soon had dry grass well ablaze. But for a camp fire logs are essential, and these could not be procured without our going through the thicket into a clump of trees which, in the darkness, was a risky proceeding. Not wishing to expose our boys to danger we made and lighted torches of long, dry grass and reeds, and armed with these, and shouting and singing, we entered the wood and soon returned laden with a plentiful supply of firewood.

During the night, a gentle, steady breeze began to blow upstream. Borne on this came the sound of hammering on the boiler of our steamer, which was receiving its finishing touches at Matope, and as the wind increased we heard voices and laughter. We shouted in unison again and again, and fired some more precious revolver shots. In vain. The breeze against us was too strong. So we made grass screens to keep off the wind, and kept the fire bright. The atmosphere seemed almost composed of mosquitoes and winged insects. All we could do was to create pungent smoke with green grass, and into the wreaths we periodically plunged our heads.

Mr. Stewart while swimming had found his pipe still in his mouth. He pocketed it, but the tobacco had gone with his coat. I, though not a smoker, sometimes carried some cigars. I found I had one in my pocket, soaked and crushed, but it gave Stewart and the boys a smoke, which was all the "food" any of us had had since lunch at one o'clock. While one was always on guard to feed the fire and give the alarm, the others tried to sleep, and gradually the night wore on and dawn appeared.

In the early morning a breeze down-river set in, and before sunrise, after carefully arranging our vocalists in strategic positions, we woke the dawn with such powerful yells that soon we rejoiced to hear an answering hallo, and some twenty minutes later saw the old, condemned dinghy appear round the bend of the river.

Rowing down to Matope, we passed several hippo, which we regarded with a new respect. Keeping nearer the bank than usual, we stepped ashore, despoiled indeed of much valuable gear but safe. Strange to say, none of us contracted fever from our adventure. Even my watch, which had stopped on its immersion, was induced to resume its usual activities.

Although next morning was Sunday (we did not sail as a rule on Sundays), we got up steam and proceeded to the scene of our adventure, hoping with a chain grapple to recover guns or gear. As we approached the place we were astonished and somewhat awed to see the head of a large crocodile keeping its position in the current right over the place of the accident. Swimming in this way is so unusual to crocodiles that we could not but think that this brute was waiting for another accident. We were correspondingly thankful to the kind Providence that had carried us through our peril unharmed. Doubtless the buffalo meat, both the big leg and smaller pieces, had helped to distract the attention of the reptiles during the previous day.

We recovered none of the gear, and the only trace of the dinghy subsequently found was in the form of some copper rivets adorning the neck of a native in the village near the cataracts.

# CHAPTER XI

TRANSPORTING A STEAMER OVER THE MOUNTAINS

About 1883 the London Missionary Society desired to forward a small steamer to Tanganyika to connect and consolidate their stations at different places near the shores of the Lake. They already had a steel boat, the 'Morning Star' which, with much labour and expense, had been transported by the Zanzibar route. The steamer, the 'Habari Ngema' (Good News), they entrusted to our Company to be delivered at the south end of Lake Tanganyika. It was given to us in plates frames, planks, and cases of engines and fittings, etc. It was difficult and anxious work transporting this mass of iron and woodwork up the Kwakwa, across to the Zambesi, by steamer to Katunga, over the sixty miles of portage to Matope, and then by steamer to the north end of Nyasa. But facilities for water and land transport on that route had already been arranged.

The last stage of over two hundred miles of mountainous country between Nyasa and Tanganyika was the most serious part of the undertaking. Beyond the first fifty or sixty miles, the best route was unknown. As already stated, Joseph Thomson and James Stewart had passed with their carriers, taking travellers' ordinary impedimenta, from lake to lake. But here we had large unwieldy plates to be transported, heavy lengths of keel-pieces, long awkward ship's frames, and worst of all, a very heavy stem and rudder frame. All were to be carried up and down the mountain sides, through narrow 18-inch native paths with long overhanging grass in the plains, and trees and undergrowth in the forest.

I had to engage carriers from four different unknown tribes, who, until they learned to trust us, would not permit carriers from other neighbouring tribes to enter and spy upon their country. From all there was the constant complaint that if they left their villages the much-dreaded Awemba tribe to the south would fall upon their wives and property and exterminate them. Some would only engage to the next village. Even when I obtained them it was not easy to induce them to lift or even touch mysterious and awkwardly shaped packages. One man loads were comparatively simple, two-men loads less so, to get four men to share a load was really difficult, but to induce eight men, untrained in carrying loads, to combine to carry the heavy stern-piece, was the crowning problem of each stage of the journey. I made two swinging yokes, which distributed the weight evenly over the eight, but they had to work together, to squeeze two abreast along single-man paths, up hill and down dale, with danger to feet and limbs if any of them stumbled. It was interesting to see how soon they perceived the practical working of lever power. It was seldom that the load reached its destination without the yokes being altered for the benefit of the more knowing carriers, whether consciously or unwittingly I could not determine.

There were many handier loads with which it would have been much easier to inaugurate a regular and permanent route, but unless these heavy pieces went with the first consignment no start could be made with the building of the steamer. On the other hand, as we were inaugurating a permanent route, we could not begin giving extravagant rates of pay. And through all, we had to acquire and retain the friendship and trust of the chiefs and people. A name for fair dealing and friendliness seemed to precede us from one village or tribe to the next, so that we were not long delayed in getting into touch with the people in front of us, and slowly, without the loss of one piece, we managed four-fifths of the route.

Livingstone had been well received by a chieftainess at the south corner of Tanganyika, and here we expected to meet the London Missionary Society's party, ready to commence building. In making for the spot we had to cross the Saisi River. Fortunately it could be crossed on a narrow bridge of tree stems six or eight feet long. (At a later date I found this river one hundred yards wide with four feet of water above the same bridge, a condition in which it would have been almost impossible to carry our unwieldy loads safely over).

Beyond this we found no trace of people or village, only black ruins of burned stockade, skeletons, hyena and desolation. For hundreds of square miles, right on to Tanganyika, an organised slave war, undertaken by the Arabs, had changed the face of the country from cultivated amenity into this devastated wilderness.

We experienced great difficulty in feeding our camp and followers, having to send back to the last villages for supplies. I remember one exceptionally trying day. In the morning when we were two days march from any village, some of the men who had agreed to carry to the Lake came to say they were going home. I reasoned with them, chaffed them, laughed at them, asked what their chief would say when they got home after leaving his friend in the bush. All seemed of no avail. They would carry the loads back, but not on. I had with me my cook and boy, and eight or ten Mandala men who would, of course, be true to me. The carriers might number over a hundred. I refused to return, and would not allow them to carry back the loads.

They started up the slope on their way home, and I and my boys sat by the loads. These men had deliberately marooned us in the bush far from civilisation, I was tempted to resort to physical force or threaten to shoot one or two of the ringleaders, but apart from the moral aspect of the matter and the high ideals governing the company, it would have meant trouble in the future and the closing of the road to unarmed carriers. We sat and I prayed.

The carriers had not reached the top of the slope about half a mile off, when they stopped and had a consultation. After a few minutes the majority returned, offering to finish the journey as they had promised. They received a warm welcome, and after storing safely the loads, which would have to be brought on later, we proceeded on our way. What brought them back? Was it mere decency, or anxiety as to what their chief might say; or was it some fear of the white man's God, whom they heard us speaking about around the camp-fires at night, and singing to in words the meaning of which they could understand but little? I know not, but was content and thankful to acknowledge the good hand of God, whom, in our small way, we were seeking to serve.

And so we reached our destination at Kasakalawa on Lake Tanganyika to find it also desolated and bare of population. Hearing that the London Missionary Society agents were at Liendwe, forty miles away in the south-west corner of the Lake,

We sent on messengers and waited for them to say where they proposed to build the steamer and to take delivery of the material. Between them and us a few miles to the south a precipitous mountain came right down into the Lake. To have continued would have entailed a climb of some thousand feet over this trackless mountain and a long journey over unknown country to the Liendwe River.

The days dragged by. To supplement our food I shot waterbuck and reedbuck till they got scared and were hard to find, and we began to be on very short commons. In the shallow sandy parts of the Lake we caught small fish, the size of whitebait, but these did not go far to feed a dozen men. I was at last asked to shoot even a crocodile, but we were not actually reduced to that strait, as a big waterbuck was secured which kept us until messengers and food arrived from the London Missionary Society. Owing to the desolation at Kasakalawa and the abundance of food in the Liendwe Valley, they had prepared to build there, and they sent their boat and dhow canoes to carry the material. I was profoundly thankful to hand over in good condition these bulky loads which had made the opening of this new route so difficult.

British attitude towards the slave trade, and pointed out how much rich country had been ruined and made uninhabitable. His attitude was that the "unbelieving" negroes had no rights and had to be made to do whatever he desired.

His wives and household had evidently dressed themselves up to impress the white man with the wealth and greatness of their master. Many looked handsome in their bright clothes and silver or brass ornaments. A few favoured ones wore shoes or sandals for the occasion, much to their discomfort and loss of buoyant carriage. They passed with lulaboing and laughter, beating and singing.

Then in hideous contrast came the loaded slaves. They trudged wearily in gangs, chained or roped together, carrying ivory or loads of food or camping gear, pots for water, tents, clothes, etc. For a seemingly interminable time they passed in dreary processions, followed at length by a large crowd of ruffians to whom no fugitive or worn-out slave need look for mercy.

We learned later that a large number of slaves and guards had been sent by another path a mile or so inland in order to escape our notice. Probably many of the slave-stick victims were sent that way.

We computed that the slaves in the caravan numbered three or four thousand. But to secure these probably as many more had been killed in the raids or left exposed and helpless to starve near their ravished homes. Of those we saw, a heavy percentage would perish as the coast was reached.

Some of the women besides their loads carried infants, but the heavier children, if they could not walk, would soon be disposed of by their captors. I noticed one oldish woman carrying in addition to her load, a biggish boy, probably her only son. I remarked that doubtless he would soon be got rid of, and so it was. Some of my men, following for a short distance in the wake of the caravan, found the boy cast aside into the bush. He was alive, but the hyenas, which we heard in greatly increased numbers that night, would soon have dispatched him had he not been rescued. He was brought into camp and ultimately we paid some natives on an island to take care of him. His mother would never know. What her thoughts were that night, when she heard the hyenas quarrelling in the wake of that dismal procession, can be better imagined than described.

If, at any time, any of us were tempted to think with longing of all that we had left at home, the consciousness that we and our Company were doing something to render such a hideous scene impossible was a splendid incentive to persevere in our work.

Now, such happenings have ceased, we trust, for ever!

---

Notes:

During the mid 19th Century, it is estimated that between 80 -100,000 Africans were sold into slavery every year. Slaves captured in the Lake Nyasa area were routinely marched across to the coast and then north to Zanzibar. From there they would be transported to Arabia or India.

On their way to the coast the slaves were forced to carry the ivory acquired by the traders for sale in Zanzibar. This practice enabled the traders to transport their ivory at little or no cost and thereby increase their profit from the sale.

The north-enders were rich in cattle, which were herded by small boys on the plains near the villages, and I have seen elephants feeding in the reeds within fifty yards of them. But if I, or one of my boys, crossed their wind even half a mile away, the elephants would instantly be on the move, and disappear, only to be seen again after long and careful tracking. As the maize and other crops ripened, the villagers kept up all-night drumming to frighten the beasts off, not always with success.

It was a wonderful country and a sportsman paradise. To the east of the Lake there rose the great chain of the Livingstone Mountains running north and south, descending at places so steeply into the deep water as almost to block a passage. To the north and north-west of the Lake were great rich alluvial plains. In these early days, when the level of Lake Nyasa was ten to fifteen feet higher than at present, there were at some parts of the coast great reedy swamps and marshes almost impassable to man and useless for canoes. So soft were they that even at the drier places a man would sink waist-deep. I have seen elephants in these marshes moving slowly, half-wading, half-swimming.

On the slightly higher plains were the native villages. The better huts were beautiful circular erections. The sides were composed of large bamboos a few inches apart but leaning outward from the perpendicular. The spaces between the bamboos were filled in with even and symmetrical "blobs" of clay. The lintels, door-posts and interior were beautifully clayed in tasteful forms. The roof, gracefully curved and finely thatched, completed a hut which was unique in grace and beauty. These huts were not crowded in a stockade, but placed separately on the open ground, with a large space in front cleanly weeded and swept, shaded by enormous india rubber trees (*Ficus indica*). All round reaching to and far beyond the next houses were miles of banana trees covering the higher ridges, all cleanly weeded and affording grateful shade for passers-by and food in plenty to the inhabitants.

In the evenings the cattle collected in the shade of the trees around the fires fed with banana-leaf or dried dung. The smoke from which they knew would protect them from the flies and "clegs" (horseflies) that plagued them sorely. They were housed at night not in open cattle kraals, but in special houses occupied at one end by the owner and his family. They were tethered to one wall, leaving a narrow passage down the other side. These houses might be forty or more feet long, according to the riches of the man, eight or ten feet broad, with rounded roofs about six or eight feet high. In shape they were not unlike a long railway carriage. The cattle were very tame, and were taught to follow their masters. It was not uncommon to see the owners running ahead, their ankle bells tinkling, and a dozen or more cattle following at a trot or gallop. This was a valuable habit, as in the event of a sudden attack made on the owner they followed him as he escaped.

Milk was largely used by the chief families, not fresh but curdled in large gourds or pots which were emptied but never washed. The fresh milk therefore curdled quickly, the cream and curd forming the top. The half-round section of a banana stem was inserted at one edge of the pot, and the whey was drained off for the boys and dogs, while the curd was eaten by the great folk. A spoon for milk, water, or other liquid was easily made from a small section of a broad banana leaf, preferably toughened by exposure for a moment to the fire. One half of the breadth was folded over on itself, making a scoop or spoon, useful in many ways.

In a country where trees are very scarce, with the exception of those cultivated for shade near the dwellings of the chiefs, the banana was used for many purposes. Though the trees, to a cursory glance, appeared very similar, they really comprised a number of varieties. Seated in the shade afforded by the great leaves, four to six feet long by one foot broad, I asked a native how many kinds he could see, and he named seven or eight different varieties which were used in different ways. There were the small and large bananas, eaten ripe in the big bunches now so familiar to people at home. They were preferably hung up in the dark to mature. The variety most commonly used for food was of medium size but astringent in taste, and reputably noxious until they had been thoroughly heated or roasted in ashes. Others were dried in the sun and eaten raw on a journey. The dried bananas or plantains were ground into meal to be cooked into nsima or porridge.

Dried banana leaves skilfully twisted together were used as fuel. A man wanting to wash his hands, would cut off part of the very succulent endogenous stem, squeeze out the juice, and perform his ablutions. Some dry leaves were used as his towel. In the absence of iron nails practically all African huts are tied together, and the fibrous bark of many forest trees used elsewhere was here replaced by the strong fibres of the banana stem. I have seen these stems used to make walls for temporary houses, and the leaves used as thatch. When we visited a chief he would usually cut a large unbroken leaf from a tree for us to sit on and where the canteen was far away, and we had no plate, a section of leaf made a capital substitute on which to lay our spatchcocked fowl.

In the country slightly lower than the banana avenues, the men, using large two-handed hoes, cultivated maize, sorghum, peas, and other vegetables; the women assisted in light work. Farther afield were great grassy and reedy plains used by the cattle, and often invaded by elephants and buffalo.

# CHAPTER XIV

### THE CROCODILE'S VICTIM

A number of rivers found their way to the Lake from the mountains beyond the Wankonde country. They were usually deep and comparatively sluggish, and abounded in large crocodiles. These rivers were from twenty to forty yards across and, being unfordable, canoes were required. Mostly these were quite safe, but there was a decided spice of danger in crossing in a canoe one of the sides of which had rotted or had broken away, for the crocodiles were aggressive. At one ford a big crocodile used to swim lazily about, waiting for accidents. His scaled hide was proof against native spears. But several of that kind troubled the fords no more after we had passed, for no animal's skin that I know of is proof against modern rifles.

On one occasion near our principal camp at the Mbashi River a man passed on his way southward. He was somewhat fuddled with native beer, and instead of going round by a ford or waiting for a canoe he started to swim across. He was nearly halfway over when he gave an exclamation and made for our side of the river at full speed. We found that a piece of the calf of his leg, about the size of an apple, had been bitten clean out. Fortunately for him it must have been a small crocodile that gave him his lesson. We washed and dressed the wound, and as the artery could be seen throbbing intact, he would have a good chance of recovery.

One season, after the news of elephants in the district had spread, we made up a party of four or five Europeans, including two officers from the Cape, Captains Fairlie and Berry. One of our favourite base camps was on the Luwaya River, in Mwakyusa's country. We pitched our tents among the bananas and were able to buy food and milk from the villagers. One attraction of the spot was the possibility of a safe bathe. A short descent from our tents led to a field of maize, beyond which flowed the deep river. In front of us, an island fifty or sixty yards long divided it into two unequal portions. There was on our side a large pool, about five or six feet deep in parts, with shallow sandbanks at the head and tail of the island. Although the main river swarmed with crocodiles we found this pool clear of them. Here we bathed practically every day, sometimes twice. Our native followers copied our example, and more often than not there were six to twenty natives frolicking about in the water.

One day we bathed and swam and dived as usual, and landed to dry and dress, Captain Berry alone lingering behind. He was quietly swimming under water when his head rose suddenly, and he uttered an exclamation that attracted our attention. He went under again immediately. The next thing we saw was an immense crocodile with his body in its jaws, mounting the sandbank at the bead of the pool and plunging into the river beyond. The ghastly affair was bewilderingly sudden, and it took us a few minutes to get rifles and cartridges from the camp. But among the crocodiles we saw swimming, none seemed to be clutching the body, as crocodiles often do. Nearly every one of any size that raised its eyes above the surface got a bullet that morning, but we could get no trace of our friend.

*Heart of Africa*

The news spread, and soon Mwakyusa, the chief, arrived. He was much distressed, and declared he would at least get the body for us. When we learned his intention we tried to dissuade him from a useless attempt. Not to be put off he and a dozen strong men armed with spears, crossed chest deep over into the deep river. With their spears they explored the steep banks under which they thought the crocodile might have hidden its prey. They were unsuccessful. Mwakyusa may have been afraid that we would hold him responsible for the death of Captain Berry by a bewitched crocodile. Yet it was a brave act for the chief to lead his men on such a perilous quest, and it gave us a new respect for him and them, for we had sometimes been inclined to think them self-indulgent and ready to hand over any dangerous work to subordinates.

Seeking an explanation of the reptile's presence in our pool, we noticed that the river was somewhat turbid instead of clear, and that the bank where we usually dressed was submerged. There must have been rain in the distant hills, which had swollen the river. The shallow banks at the head and tail of our pool were therefore deeper, and the reptile had entered it by night. Invisible in the turgid waters it had lain close to our feet till the splashing and frolicking had ceased and one doomed man was alone. So simple a circumstance, and yet it meant the life of a friend.

For years one could hardly bear to think of it, still less to tell of it, but distance and time tend to blunt the keenest of feelings.

# CHAPTER XV

### MY FIRST ELEPHANT

One's first elephant is a great occasion. Books written by South African hunters advise waiting till elephants get into the forest as in the grass there is danger to hunter and his horse. In Nyasaland, horses are practically non-existent on account of the tsetse fly, and it was only on extraordinary occasions that elephants were found in the woods.

The home of the Central African elephant by day was in the long grass of the plains, eight or ten feet high, alternatively among the fifteen to twenty-foot reeds and the thickets of the swamps. When marching through the grass the hunter could not see them. From the side of a hill (if there was one) or a tree, or the top of an ant-heap, one could scan the plains. Far away would appear some dark objects. They might be rocks, or bushes, or possibly buffalo in shorter grass. If white birds were seen fluttering over them the probability was that large game was there. If, further on, one could distinguish the slow flap of great ears fanning the huge bodies the excitement began. If, in addition, one or two trunks were seen held aloft, sniffing the breeze, the greatest caution had to be exercised, and a long detour was necessary to ensure an approach upwind. Should the scent of a hunter reach them, even a mile away, the probability was great that long before the stalking was accomplished the elephants would be off

On the occasion of my first elephant I was told by the chief that a herd had recently been on a certain plain. Every preparation having been made, I took my favourite double-barrelled 12-bore Henry rifle, and a 500-express in reserve, and started after breakfast. Besides the trackers, who often, had to noiselessly press aside the tall grass to let me pass. I had four or five of my own men armed with muzzle-loaders in case of a charge.

From a tree we saw at least one elephant out in the plain and started for it. The wind being favourable, we were able to follow game or cattle paths for a time and at length reached a deep ditch beyond which was our quarry. A native got quietly into the water and inserting his head between my legs, soon landed me on the other side not far from where the elephant had been seen. The began the stalk proper. Each step had to be noiseless, all cracking of twigs or dry grass being avoided.

Gently pressing aside the grass, we approached the spot where we had seen him. Would he be gone? Would he be alone? If we fired at one, what would the rest of the herd do? Startled by the shot, would they scatter or possibly charge us? A full grown elephant is a mountain of bone and muscle, ten to twelve feet high and has a long heavy trunk, a mere tap from which can lay one senseless. With it also a man can be seized and dashed to the ground, where he is trampled to death or gored with the great gleaming tusks. How would he be standing? Possibly with his great stern towards us, where no sure shot could be got and if so, would we be able to creep back and make a new approach? All sorts of questions passed through the mind in these minutes.

# CHAPTER XII

### THE SLAVE CARAVAN

It was at Kasakalawa that I encountered the largest slave caravan I ever saw. Kabunda, probably the despoiler of the country I had passed through, had strong fortified villages in the Liendwe Valley not many miles from the London Missionary Society's station~ He cultivated large tracts of land by means of his slaves, and there at any rate for a time was peace and plenty. The native villages in the valley were not raided, but were rather protected by him.

When the time came to make his journey to the coast of Zanzibar, he secretly made his preparations. Then he sent out his ruga-ruga (warriors) to surround the native villages and capture all the men, women and children with whom he had lived on terms of friendship. It was a splendid haul ready to his hand.

The strong men most liable to escape or cause trouble were fastened in a gori or slave-stick, consisting of a straight tree or branch, seven or eight feet long by four or five inches diameter, divided into a fork at the thinner end. The slave's neck was inserted into this fork, and a rod of iron driven through the two ends and riveted there, leaving only sufficient room for the neck. A string was attached to the butt end of the stick, and this, fastened to a tree, kept him safe; or, tied to a high branch, pinned him to the ground at night. The strings of two gories tied together near the forks prevented the gories from trailing on the ground, and allowed the two wearers to march eight or ten feet apart, and also to carry the load of ivory or food assigned to them. Other slaves were secured in strong iron collar-rings riveted on their necks and fastened at intervals of a few feet on a long chain. Some of the women were bound to strong bark ropes, while others, not likely to attempt to escape, were allowed to carry their loads unchained, but were closely guarded by armed men.

Any attempt to escape or to linger on the march speedily brought on the offender, man or woman, such punishment from hippo-hide whips as to compel obedience. Those who were refractory or unable to carry the loads were, after brutal treatment, brained, and left at the side of the road, to inspire others with fear and dread. Children able to walk followed their mothers. What was done with slave infants whose mothers had to carry heavy loads can be surmised.

We heard of their approach a day before they reached us. Doubtless our camp had already been carefully spied upon, and they were satisfied that two white men and a dozen natives were unable to interfere with a caravan of several Arabs with hundreds of fierce, well-armed ruga-ruga in attendance. A small party came on ahead to inform us of their approach and to profess friendship. Soon the advance guard of the ruga-ruga appeared brandishing their weapons as they passed along the sands of the lake-shore in front of our little encampment.

Then the chief Kabunda himself came in sight, riding on a richly-caparisoned white Muscat donkey, with a red embroidered flat saddle. He gave us a milk goat and professed friendship, but I spoke to him very plainly on the

# CHAPTER XIII

### A WONDERFUL COUNTRY

With our meagre means of communication ivory was almost the only commodity that could be profitably exported from such far inland districts as those bordering Lake Nyasa and Tanganyika. A fertile source of supply was found among the Wankonde at the north end of Lake Nyasa.

These Wankonde, a brave and warlike set of tribes under Mwakyusa, Mankenja, and Manjawara, had, with their spears and shields, maintained the independence of their country against Arabs and Angoni. Their clothing was scanty, consisting chiefly of a belt of cord closely wound round with thin brass wire. The more important men would wear eight or ten such belts. When visiting a European, a section of a banana leaf, or a bunch of leaves or grass suspended by the waist cord, completed the toilet. Many, especially chiefs sons, wore anklets of similar make-up with tinkling iron bells attached. A large -bladed stabbing spear, half a dozen villainously barbed throwing-spears, a knobkerrie, and narrow hide shield on a wicker frame, comprised their fighting equipment. When one saw a chiefs son in the prime of young manhood, accompanied by six to twenty followers, bounding along in step, the thud of the bare feet and the tinkling bells keeping perfect time, on could not but admire the muscular frames, the erect carriage and the poetry of motion which they displayed. A dozen bands of such young warriors approaching at full speed from as many different directions with hostile intent would constitute a very awkward proposition.

We had been warned that the north-enders were treacherous and untrustworthy, but I lived among them for several periods of two or three months each, once alone, and retained their friendship and goodwill to the end. This was fortunate, for, as will be seen, it was they who, when the Arabs in overwhelming force attacked and laid siege to our station at Karonga, sent down a band of many hundred warriors and raised the siege. The chiefs dubbed me " father of the tribes". (In 1914, when the Germans, to whom the sovereignty of that district had been assigned after the Berlin Conference, were fighting against the British, these chiefs sent messages through the missionaries, asking why I would not return and take over the country which so long ago belonged to me!)

On visiting them we bought some ivory, and were given a very cordial invitation to shoot elephants, which at that time were the plague of the country. As they had practically no guns their miles of banana plantations and other cultivations were at the mercy of any passing herd. I saw the result of one night's visit. In an acre or two of bananas, under the cooling and grateful shade of which we had been accustomed to pass, hardly one tree remained standing. Deigning to eat only the most succulent young shoots and leaves at the heart of the plants, they had ruthlessly smashed down and scattered everytree, so that the way was completely blocked. Many a family's food was destroyed, and a year or two would pass before new shoots came into bearing.

Then hazily, through the long grass not ten feet away, I became aware of the huge bulk. I crept a little nearer and there he stood, side and foreleg visible. The African elephant's enormous ear, when laid back against his side, covers his foreleg and if he is standing broadside on, a shot through the edge of it, at the right height, is almost sure to reach the heart. One more moment of silence and then the thunder of my 12-bore rent the stillness! All was confusion. He did not turn on us, but made off and I gave him my second barrel, reloaded and followed. He had not gone one hundred yards when we heard a heavy crash, and when we came up we found him already dead.

Up rushed one of my boys and cut off the tail, to be preserved as a valuable trophy. Soon the natives from the adjoining villages, attracted by the firing, joined the group, and great joy was manifested at the death of a marauding enemy and equally the prospect of great quantities of food from the mountainous carcass before them.

The hunters first secured what was wanted for the camp, and then the villagers set to work in earnest, using all kinds of spears. Soon several men were inside the animal, cutting and hacking, and throwing their spoil to their women, who carried off in their baskets what had been secured. What a babel of voices! What a scramble! No wonder tempers were not always serene, often the contents of the entrails were used as missiles against a neighbour. As one after another of the principal hackers emerged to get a breath of air, they presented a weird spectacle, breathless, perspiring, covered with blood and fat, their eyes gleaming with excitement and pleasure, and their faces suffused with an exultant grin. As more villagers arrived, the hubbub increased, and village rivalry developed till the uproar could be heard miles away down the wind.

At length the great limbs were severed and carried off. The huge trunk, carried so tightly and used so nimbly by the elephant, required five or six men to carry it. It went probably to the chief. In an hour or two little remained except the great head and tusks, and the contents of the stomach. The bones, the skin even, had been cut up and carried away to villages far and near.

The removal of the tusks from the skull was a difficult and delicate business. Strongly imbedded for a third of their length in the hard bones of the upper jaw, the dentist required strong and heavy instruments. The skin and flesh having been removed and the skull turned up, one of the principal hunters chopped away the bone surrounding the tusk with the heaviest axe procurable. A skilful, neat-handed man planting his heavy blows at the exact spot may, with a good axe, cut out even a large tusk in five or ten minutes. With an inferior weapon, or an unskilled workman, it may be a long process. The ivory being so much harder than the bone, the tusk, with careful handling, will emerge free from cut or scratch. An amateur, on the other hand, may chip and scar it badly. A full grown elephant's tusk is usually hollow for about a third of its length, corresponding roughly with the part that is enclosed in the bones of the head. This hollow is filled with a soft, somewhat gelatinous nerve. As only the senior hunters are supposed to see and remove this, the initiated carry off the tusks to some little distance, loosen with the finger or a knife the cartilage from the thin edge of the tusk Then shake out the nerve, and bury it or hide it from the rest of the party.

Hardly had the last man left the place than vultures descended first singly, then in twos and threes in short, quick spirals, until dozens were fighting over the scraps that were left.

I have often been asked if the flesh of the elephant is good. It is certainly wholesome, as the animal is a clean feeder. A big tusker, the coveted ambition of the hunter, being old and muscular, is naturally tough and hard. But his trunk, if cooked sufficiently long and slowly, is capital eating. On one occasion a piece of such a trunk was buried in a hole full of ashes below a camp fire, which was continuously kept burning for three nights and two days to dry the meat and I found it most delicate and appetising. Next day a chief, instead of bringing a fowl as a present, or for sale (much the same thing), sent one of his wives with a native clay-pot of stewed elephant. As a matter of courtesy I took a morsel expecting it to be somewhat of the consistency of leather. But it must also have been simmering for a couple of days and nights properly attended to, and it was delicious tender and juicy, so I had it for supper. Younger bulls and cows are naturally more tender. From a fat elephant, and some are fat, one can easily get a bucket or two of the finest lard, a valuable asset to the kitchen.

Incidentally, this elephant had the longest tail-hairs I ever saw. They measured twenty-seven inches instead of the usual six to ten inches. To unbelievers I can say I've got the tail, and can produce it.

# CHAPTER XVI

### A BIG BAG

The tackling of a large herd of elephants presents peculiar difficulties. To secure a big bull is often hazardous. Some of the smaller ones may be wandering away from the herd feeding, and if one is disturbed, the whole will be gone almost instantaneously. Even after the hunter gets near, the cows may hide a vital spot in the tusker. Hence patience is necessary. Then, while waiting, a change in the wind may spoil the whole day's sport. When at last the first shot is fired there will probably be a stampede of the herd, hither and thither, to the great danger of the hunters.

If no elephant falls, then the slow process of tracking follows. The herd (unless there are badly wounded amongst them) usually unite in their flight and keep together in a mad rush for half a mile. Woe betide any one who is in their way at such a moment! The tall grass or reeds are flattened for a width of ten or fifteen feet as if by a steamroller, so there is no trouble in following at the double. But you must keep your eyes open lest your wounded bull may have strayed to one side and be waiting to deal with you as you hurry on. As he catches sight of his puny tormentors, out go his great ears, forward comes his massive trunk, and with a shrill trumpet down he comes. Picture that agile monster; twelve feet high, ten feet between the edges of his great rounded outstretched ears, his solid gleaming tusks, his mobile, prehensile trunk, his little eyes burning with rage, his huge depth and weight approaching like a monster railway engine. What can repel his irresistible charge?

However the attackers are armed with the products of science, and provided there be no misfire at the critical moment, a 12-bore rifle bullet between the eyes for the brain, or, in his chest for his heart usually brings him to a standstill.

The native hunters and gun bearers are remarkably quick on such occasions. They can dive head first into the long grass in a way impossible to those better clad. On one occasion one of them nearly suffered for his pride. Clothing must be as inconspicuous as possible, but Maso arrayed himself, contrary to instructions, in a clean, white loincloth. Chased by an elephant he dived into the grass, but it caught sight of the cloth and seized it with its trunk and brandished it aloft. Fortunately the twisted knot gave way, and a very subdued and frightened Maso emerged later from the grass unhurt. There was no need thereafter to insist on white loincloths being taboo!

We found in the early days that a herd, even after being fired on, would usually stop a mile or two farther on. So leaving one or two boys to look after any first bag, we would follow at full speed in its wake. It took all the excitement of the chase to carry us over these sunny, hot plains, for the tall grass shut out any breeze. Carrying a light rifle and followed closely by a boy with my heavy one, I would run, perspiring, thirsty, but eager to come up with the quarry. Then the spoor would show that the elephants were no longer in a solid herd but were scattering. Swerving to right or left to secure a good approach with the best wind, we would try to get within firing distance again, or send natives ahead to drive them down in our direction. In this way we would get another elephant or two, and then, tired out but triumphant, give up the chase.

Our commissariat department was sometimes able to follow us, and food and tea were wonderfully refreshing, but at other times it would lose our tracks. In that case we would be fortunate if we were within reasonable distance of a village where we could secure bananas and milk. Sometimes we were far afield, amid miles of plains, and with the minimum of shade. If we came across a pool of water we strained the liquid through cloth before drinking, but occasionally the only moisture available was in the marshy ground at the bottom of deep holes made by elephant's feet. Exhausted and almost fainting, after an exciting and successful hunt, I remember on one occasion cutting a long, grass straw, and drinking some of that marshy liquid. Strange to say it did me no harm.

Here are some entries, by way of illustration, from one of my old notebooks:

*Sunday, 6th November.* Before breakfast, elephants reported just across Mbashi, so gave orders for a start, forgetting it was Sunday, but countermanded when found out. Hoped they would stay for us.

*Monday, 7th November.* Elephants had crossed Mbashi, and were visible within five hundred yards distance of house, so they had stayed for us indeed. A three miles' walk round brought us to them, and we posted parties to drive them through a marsh towards our house. We stalked, and fired, getting three soon after the first volley. Drivers did not keep them down-river, but they made a long circle and crossed above us. I reached them after a long run, as they were halfway across, and got a good many shots into them, disabling one good one, but could not manage to finish him for a long time. The others escaped and went towards the Lake. In all we got seven, and went back, partly by canoe, very pleased.

Had some very comforting egg-flip, milk and bananas, and saying if the elephants would only come back here we would waken them up. Just then a cloud of dust appeared, and the elephants, followed by two boys, came in sight, making direct for us, or rather for the plain on other side of river. We called together what guns there were andcrossed in an old canoe. Lost sight of them for some time, but they appeared again, and away we went through the marsh over floating grass. Fenwick fired first, and down his went. I got a good tusker about centre of herd and two shots floored it. Fairley got up next to the line, and with two shots brought down the leader, and gave it a third shot in the head as it lay to make sure of it.

When we came back to these three 'dead' ones, we found only one remained, and it was moving its head and ears, and required four more shots to kill it. The other two had made off and one was shot subsequently. The remaining beast had been fired at again, and turning back the way it had come met Vigerona, who had originally driven them down to us. It caught hold of his gun, a 6-bore, by the small of the butt and shied it to a distance, breaking the doghead, his 8-bore cartridges being finished, he was left without a gun. Meantime we pursued at racing speed. Some of the elephants broke off, with Fenwick and the boys after them. I followed the herd, and we got two more, in all eight. So that the days work amounted to fifteen elephants, a good many of them being bulls with good or fair tusks. So much for waiting over Sunday. We returned tired, but elephants being so near the door we were not done out but in great spirits.

*Tuesday, 8th November.* Gave whole crowd of boys 1 quarter fathoms of American sheeting, also needles and thread, so all in high spirits.

*Wednesday, 9th November.* Sent for tusks. In afternoon Fairley and I went to see elephant that died in the Mbashi: a lot of large crocodiles about; shot one.

*Thursday, 10th November.* Susi brought word that another elephant had died at Mwakyusa's, and brought in two small elephant tusks. That makes sixteen elephants for one day.

It was the biggest number of elephants secured in one day. So we lost nothing by obeying the good old rule of resting on Sunday, although a good many hard and foolish things had been said that Sunday morning when I called the hunt off. The satisfaction at the bag was not confined to the hunters. Men, women and children by the thousand appeared from villages near and far, to cut up and carry off the spoil. It was a time of great rejoicing. For never before had so many of the people had meat in such abundance, and there would also be sixteen fewer elephants to raid the defenceless gardens. By the third day hardly a liftable bone or bit of skin was left for the vultures and hyenas to quarrel over.

The recollection of crossing the deep, crocodile-infested rivers on floating grass sometimes even now causes a shudder, but when following elephants what will a young and strong man not dare in order to get up to the quarry? If the vegetation supports a man while the elephants have to plough their way through it, he gains on them, but it is a risky proceeding. I once, near the north east corner of the Lake, encountered a herd of bulls, which were impeded by swamps and deep channels with floating grass. In this I and my boys in crossing sank sometimes waist-deep. I got one bull with 83 and 84lb. tusks, two with tusks over 60 lb. each, and two between 30 and 40 lb. a very valuable bag for one forenoon. The big bull had the heaviest tusks I ever secured by shooting.

All this ivory went without deduction to the credit of the Company. Indeed, in these early days, when we were so heavily handicapped by the deterioration of the steel hull of our first steamer, the large sums realised for ivory did much to keep the Company in funds, and so enabled it to carry on the work for which it had been founded.

# CHAPTER XVII

### TAMING YOUNG ELEPHANTS

From the first, we laid plans to capture and tame young elephants for our work. Overland transport had for long been undertaken by native porters. Horses, and to a lesser extent, donkeys and mules, soon succumbed to the bite of the tse-tse fly. Elephants were considered immune from this pest. If we could secure sufficient to carry loads overland between the navigable reaches, the knell of the slave trade would soon be rung. Indian wild elephants are captured in keddahs, but trained hunters, and especially tame elephants, are required to secure and subjugate them. We had neither. So we were resigned to endeavouring to secure young elephants which could be reared and taught.

One day after a big shoot we found a young elephant near its dead mother. The natives wanted to kill and enjoy the juicy morsel, but I forbade it, and offered a weeks pay to the brave who would secure the youngster. Several men essayed the task, but when surrounded it raised its little trunk and dashed at its nearest adversary, who bolted. The cordon had to be re-formed. I joined the hunters when the circle was small, and slipping up from behind got my arm round its neck behind its big ears, and seizing his trunk with my left hand held on. Then began a tug-of-war, but the men closed in, held on to his legs and tail, and we threw him. In order to tie him up and lead him away, we cut reims from his mother's ears. With a strong strap round his neck held by two men, and two others holding a cord on his two hind feet to act as a brake and with myself behind his ears and holding his trunk, we set out for camp, two miles off. It was a fight all the way, and we arrived pretty well exhausted.

We tied up our little captive and sent to a neighbouring village for a bucket of fresh milk. However it would not drink from a basin or bucket. We took our india rubber filter-tube and steeped it in milk, and then syphoned a little into its mouth. As soon as the thirsty little tongue tasted the liquid the difficulty was over, and just as quickly as the tube could pass the milk it disappeared. The poor animal, however, did not take to captivity, and though well fed with milk, it died in a week or so.

When some weeks later we had the chance of another young elephant, we determined to secure him. As he was considerably bigger and stronger than the last, we were all the more hopeful. However you have first to catch your elephant before you can tame him. It was a long and hard repetition of our former experience, but in the end we secured him, got him tied up, and began the journey back. Attempts to escape were numerous, refusals to proceed as common, but my right hand was firmly round his neck, and my left hand held his trunk as a sort of rudder, and so we laboriously proceeded.

Late in the afternoon we reached our destination, and tied up our captive to an india rubber tree we had recently transplanted to provide shade. Being somewhat exhausted by the long struggle in the hot afternoon sun, I was taking a few minutes rest, prior to feeding him, when an uproar arose in the camp and a boy rushed in to say the elephant had pulled up the, tree by the root, and dragging it after him, was chasing everyone round the camp. As the tree hampered his progress, he was easily secured and fastened to the doorpost of a hut which he could not move. Milk and the filter-tube were soon ready. We got him to taste the liquid, and then with his trunk up in the air he was ready for a feed.

With the tube between the first and second fingers of my left hand I thrust my hand into his mouth. Crunch went his teeth, and I speedily withdrew a maimed hand. The nail of my middle finger was hanging by two threads, and there was a deep gash in front of it. A bruised wound of this kind is liable to give trouble in Central Africa, and there was no one able to render much assistance. Strips from a boiled handkerchief were used to bind up the wound, but it was desirable to have some substitute for oil-silk to prevent the dressing from drying too hard. Having been experimenting with the juice of the india rubber plant (*Ficus indica*), I found the latex coagulated into hard cakes. These, when put into hot water, became soft and pliable like gutta-percha, and could then be stretched into fine tissue. I accordingly heated some of the cakes I had beside me and soon had a very creditable dressing. The wound healed up in time, although thirty five years later the injury may still be traced on nail and finger.

Meantime the elephant remained unfed. Appeals to my boys and hunters were unavailing; if the savage beast had bitten their master, it would kill them! So I started again. Allowing the tube to protrude far beyond the fingers of my right hand, and not allowing them far into the mouth, we presently established a satisfactory working arrangement, and a basin full of milk speedily disappeared.

We found he was very fond of young bango reeds, certain classes of swamp grass which grew in abundance along the shore and of sweet potatoes, of which we could purchase any quantity. We made him a round house strong enough to prevent him wandering and able to resist a night attack by lions. By day he was usually tethered near my house.

One morning we thought we had lost him, as he got loose and bolted. Trackers were put on, and he was soon located near some villages. He was captured and brought back, and thereafter accepted the situation and remained quietly with us. Probably he realised that without the protection of his mother he was helpless in the open, and was glad of our care and attention. Almost every young elephant we caught made in one way or another a dash for liberty, and thereafter seemed ready to accept the inevitable.

Very soon we became great friends, so much so that he was given the name 'Billy'. He would follow me like a dog, and, finding I often carried sweet potatoes in my pocket, his agile little trunk would extract them for himself. He might almost have been given his liberty to go where he liked, but in that case our food supply would have been seriously curtailed.

The native women from the villages brought flour and potatoes for sale every morning. Billy's appearance created a panic among them, and they would drop their baskets and run off screaming, leaving our young friend to feed on the best. A miniature charge, with ears outspread and trunk aloft, would send off any native at the run. So he had to be tied up except when out with his master or his native keeper.

He was strong enough to carry me on his back, and showed no objection to my mounting him, but as he was young, I only made the experiment once or twice. He throve well even when I was absent for a day or two, but a month or so later, when far away from headquarters, I had a message that Billy was sick. I hurried back, but only to find my dear little companion dead. The natives were fond of and understood and appreciated their cattle, but had quite a different feeling towards 'wild things of the forest', which they regarded as in another category. I did not find any dereliction of duty on the part of the keepers, but I question if they ever had any affection for the animal.

# CHAPTER XVIII

### SMALLER GAME

Every pioneer and explorer in a new country is bound at times to rely on his gun for feeding himself and his men. On elephant hunting expeditions we often preferred to go on short commons rather than fire at smaller game and possibly frighten our quarry. On one occasion, after several days unsuccessful tramps after elephant, we decided we must get some food, so we stalked a large herd of buffalo in a grassy plain. With a favourable wind two of us crept up under cover of some patches of grass, close to the great bull sentinels. These had wonderful horns, massive and rugged, but as their flesh would be rank and tough, we chose two young animals in the herd, and fired simultaneously. Only one fell. Mine galloped off with the herd but soon dragged behind, and we followed to give it the coup de grace. Soon it stopped with head drooping, seemingly about to fall. As we got nearer it raised its head, saw us, and with all the fire of youth and anger, charged straight down on me. Waiting till it was within twenty yards, I fired my single-barrelled express at its forehead, expecting to drop it dead. But it came on seemingly unharmed, and the bystanders averred that I made remarkably good time clearing out before It. It was a thrilling moment. Another shot from one of our men brought it down, and we proceeded to investigate why my shot had not stopped it. The bullet had entered the centre of the forehead, but as the buffalo had lowered its head to impale me on its horns, it had gone through its gullet, just missing the brain. A charging buffalo should have been shot higher up through the horns, which, strong as they are, would not turn a powerful rifle bullet at short range.

Buffaloes are very fierce and much feared by natives.1 To follow a wounded one by its blood spoor through long grass or reeds is one of the most dangerous things a hunter may be called on to do. For, added to its great strength, it seems to possess a malicious cunning. Once, in the Elephant Marsh, we were silently and painstakingly following a wounded bull by indications of blood on the ground or on the grass, when a movement to our left startled us. In a moment, crashing through, what to us was an impenetrable wall of grass and reeds, came the wounded buffalo right upon us. It was a narrow escape. Fortunately the native tracker disappeared ahead at the first sound, and a rifle bullet at very close quarters finished the bull's career. We found he had run off straight for a considerable distance, then had made a large half circle to the left, and was standing waiting for us as we followed his spoor.

Rhinoceroses seemed to have been scarcer in Nyasaland than farther North or South, and I only bagged three.

In the early days great schools of hippopotami were a grave source of danger to boats and canoes, and I shot many. On my long exploring and trading expeditions, I also bagged eland, hartebeest, koodoo, waterbuck, and other smaller game. Lions in my time, while numerous, were not aggressive, they became so only after the rinderpest had killed so much of the game that they were driven by hunger to attack.

---

Notes:

1. It is a fact that African Buffaloes account for the majority of human deaths attributed to wild animals.

# CHAPTER XIX

### A REBELLION

In 1883 I was about to get a long-looked-for holiday to the old country, and to lay before the Board various schemes for development. My steamer ticket was taken, and all preparations made, when news of serious native disturbances reached Quilimane. Small affairs between the Portuguese and natives were not uncommon, but this rising seemed to belong to another category. As the Machinjiri to the east of the Shire and south of the Ruo were involved, our steamer communication with Blantyre and Lake Nyasa was threatened. Successive reports came in of Portuguese stations being evacuated and looted. Both banks of the Shire were occupied by the natives, while in augmented numbers they moved down the north bank of the Zambesi.

Matters looked grave, and the Portuguese were such perturbed. Some who were able took steamer to Mozambique, others made preparations to find a refuge on some sailing vessels lying in the river. Meetings were called by the authorities, but very little was done. So far, we had not heard that any except Portuguese had been molested, but when their soldiers, after a fight, had been driven from Mopea, it was reported that the local natives were joining the rebels. It became necessary to assure the safety of our station at Marum on the Zambesi, where our steamer was lying with some passengers. Not only were British people in danger, but the oil-seed buying agencies of the French and Dutch houses on the Zambesi were menaced. We accordingly called a meeting of the non-Portuguese Europeans, and planned an expedition to the disturbed districts for the rescue of our friends and property.

We got seventeen volunteers, comprising many nationalities, British, French, Dutch, Germans, Poles and Swiss, including the chief agents of the French and Dutch houses. All our own staff volunteered and as both in men and in interests we outnumbered the others, I was chosen leader. There was a babel of languages, but fortunately I could communicate with them all in one tongue or another. We got ready any useful rifles and ammunition we had, and raised two or three swords. We were, however, very short of guns for our natives, who would be required first to row the boats up the Kwakwa and then to act as a bodyguard in any succeeding action. The Portuguese gave us their cordial blessing, and, what was more to the point, lent us some guns and ammunition. We raised about a dozen houseboats, and some large canoes for the natives and impedimenta. Including natives we were under a hundred all told.

With double crews we made all haste. It was very anxious work in the upper reaches of the Kwakwa, where perfect ambuscades could, at various places, have fired on us at point-blank range. Some refugees from Mopea who passed on the way to Quilimane told us that so far as they knew, the rebels, while they had captured the Portuguese fort there, had not yet reduced the opium company's station situated between Mopea and the Zambesi. We learned that several Portuguese and one Scotsman, Robert Henderson, formerly an African Lakes Company's man, but then chief engineer to that Portuguese company, were defending the fortified station, and that they were hard pressed. The main body of the enemy was detained there.

As Portuguese Mopea was in the hands of the rebels, we disembarked at Marendinny early one morning and made our way in three divisions under the principal men, towards the opium factory, by native paths through the long grass. It was not known what attitude the workers at the factory were taking, but while still some miles from our destination, we were glad to hear sounds of firing, indicating that the fort had not yet been captured. We hurried on, the long grass preventing our seeing more than a few yards before us, and it was not till we reached the cultivated land that any fighting was visible. The station lay less than a mile away, and it was swarming with natives who were firing into it from close quarters, the outer walls and stockade having been entered. To our right ran a stream, in the direction of the fort, on our side of which was a ridge whence we could see fairly well.

We divided our party, two bands advancing from points to the left, while we kept along the ridge. A number of armed natives approached on the other side of the stream, and were thought by our natives to be friendlies. We signalled to them to join us, but they knelt down, and at about one hundred yards range opened fire. Fortunately we had cover behind our ridge, and we returned their fire to such good purpose that we put them to flight. We then advanced steadily towards the station amid a good deal of sniping from both sides. This bold advance into the open of three parties led by whites seems to have been a new experience to the enemy, as they had hitherto advanced practically unopposed. Our long-range rifle bullets began to reach them, and we were pleased to see them gradually withdrawing towards the Zambesi. It was the first check on their hitherto victorious progress.

We made our way into the station and found we were none too early. After a brave defence of the outer stockade our friends had taken refuge in a building, the lower storey of which was of stone, the second storey and the roof of corrugated iron. From this point of vantage they had succeeded in keeping the stockade clear. The iron walls were riddled with bullets, but bales and bags inside formed a protection.

Henderson, who had been the leader of the defence, had been shot in the cheek, and was becoming weak. Ammunition was nearly exhausted. The assailants had gained the compound, and one of the Portuguese had stationed himself with a hatchet at the top of the stair to defend the party to the last. Unable otherwise to reduce the house, the attacking natives had begun to bring up firewood, stored for the use of the agricultural engines, and heap it against the strong wooden door to burn it down. Only the sharp crack of our rifles at a distance brought the besieged a message of hope.

Needless to say, we received a warm welcome on our timely arrival, and, under protection of the stockade, I held a council of war. We were hopelessly outnumbered, and so it was important to press our initial advantage before the foe could learn how few we were.

They also were engaged in a council of war, as from the high buildings we could see them closely grouped together. Selecting all whom I considered good shots with long-range rifles, and sighting at 1200 yards, we fired several volleys into them. We must have done important damage, for the natives, not improbably thinking the rain of bullets from an incredible distance to be some new form of white man's magic, scattered and gradually disappeared. We watched carefully lest they might not be making a dash to rush the stockade, but they did not attack. We posted sentries to guard against a night assault. Next morning we found they were in full retreat, and had already covered many miles homewards. Had the rebels got past Mopea, the Portuguese feared they would be joined by all the Zambesi and Quilimane natives who had little cause to love their masters.

We found that our agent and the passengers on the steamer at Maruru, about ten miles down the Zambesi, were unharmed. Naturally they were in great anxiety and had been ready, if necessary, to take the steamer downriver in hope of rescue arriving from some unknown source.

So far so good, but the Zambesi and Shire would require to be opened to navigation before I could think of resuming my interrupted journey home. The natives at the important town of Sena on the Zambesi, a few miles west of the entrance into it of the Shire, had not joined in the insurrection, but were naturally in a disturbed state. As the Dutch and French houses had stations on the Zambesi as far up as Sena, we embarked their agents on the '*Lady Nyasa*' with our armed men, and proceeded thither. We received a warm welcome, and the news of the native retreat brought relief to the authorities.

Returning to Maruru, we landed all foreigners and with mails and goods started for the Shire, exclusively a British expedition, to open navigation through the country of the natives with whom we had been fighting. The expedition was hazardous, even for a small steamer. At many places the channel passes close to high banks, where a determined force of natives could easily have effectually blocked the navigable passage. Any bullet could have pierced the shell plates of the lightly built steamer. All of our available staff volunteered for service, the native crew, as usual, willing to follow the lead. We were four whites. and about twenty natives all told, armed with the rifles used at Mopea.

On the second day, near Morambala, we passed one of our wooding stations, burned out. Shortly after, on a high bank to our right, we came on a large number of natives ready to dispute the passage to all passing into the heart of their country. With bales and bags forming some protection on the flat deck, we approached within speaking distance and asked for a mrandu (council) with their chief. We assured them there were no Portuguese on board, and that we were British only, passing up the river to Blantyre. Their chief, fearing capture, declined to come on board the steamer, so I offered to go ashore along with one native as interpreter, to a given point some distance off but commanded by the rifles on the steamer, to confer with the chief and two of his men.

Leaving my rifle, but with a revolver in my pocket, I landed some distance farther downstream and proceeded to the point indicated, where I was met by the chief and his two men. I emphasised, that we were quite distinct from the Portuguese, that we had always been friendly and fair to them, so why then had they burned down our wooding station and destroyed our goods?

They acknowledged that it was quite true, but that they had been maltreated and cheated by the Portuguese, and recently we had been fighting against them.

I retorted that they knew we did not wish to be unfriendly, much the reverse, but what could we do if they destroyed our property and endangered the lives of our people?

After a long palaver, we got the chief into better humour, and offered to overlook what his party had done to us if the river were again left free for our steamer and boats and if his people would prepare firewood and provisions for sale as usual.

During the palaver, the natives, by ones and twos, had approached to hear what was taking place, till there was quite a crowd surrounding our party of two. This disquieted our men on the steamer, who stood with loaded rifles behind the paddle-boxes ready to avenge any treachery. Fortunately the negotiations took a favourable turn, and it was with a great sense of relief that we parted friends, with communications to the interior stations once more open.

Both sides kept the bargain made, and we had no further trouble with these natives. Peace having been re-established, I was able to resume my interrupted journey home.

Back in Edinburgh, in addition to attending to the needs of the Company there, I was fortunate in securing as lifepartner, to accompany me back to Central Africa, a daughter of Gilbert Beith, M.P. for the Inverness Burghs. We sailed for Africa in April 1885, our departure being hurried to enable me to take part in securing treaties with native chiefs, with the view of getting British protection for the country.

## CHAPTER XX

### AN INVASION AND A MURDER

About a year later the Portuguese organised a strong military force under Major Serpa Pinto, and swept through the country, subduing it as far as the river Ruo, at that time their recognised boundary. Having overcome the Machinjiri, they resolved to occupy the country and claim sovereignty over the Makololo and the Shire Highlands, including Blantyre and Mandala. They were opposed by Chief Mlauri, who refused to retire, although we advised him to do so. He was defeated, and the Portuguese crossed the Ruo and occupied Chiromo.

Mr. John Buchanan, acting British Consul, and my brother on behalf of the Company, called a meeting of Makololo chiefs, including Ramakukan, Kasisi, the paramount chief, Masea and Katunga, to consult how the invasion should best be met. The chiefs were asked to retire without fighting the Portuguese, with a promise that losses incurred by them should be made good by the British. The chief's intention, however, was to accept a Portuguese flag, from Major Pinto, intending, if the British Queen's forces came later, to return to her sovereignty.

From this point of view Buchanan failed to move them. He then turned to my brother and urged him to do his best. He began, in Chinyanja, to remind them of their master,

Ngake (Dr. Livingstone), and his instructions to hold the country for the British who were now here. He pointed out that flags could not be changed in the way they proposed. The King of Portugal lived in friendship with our Queen, and if they voluntarily took his flag, she would say: "My friends the Makololo want to become subjects of my friend the King of Portugal, well and good." Thus they would have no opportunity of remaining or becoming British subjects. He personally guaranteed that all damage done by the invaders would be made good by the Company. "Come right away with us," he said, and "all will be well."

After further consultation they agreed, and proceeded first to Mandala and thence to Zomba.

Meantime cablegrams reporting the situation had been sent home by Consul O'Neill, of Mozambique; and Lord Salisbury, on the urgent representation of a meeting of friends of Nyasaland at home, requested Portugal to withdraw Serpa Pinto from the Makololo country.

On their stalling, he recalled Sir Edward Malet, the British Ambassador at Lisbon, and sent a British man-of-war to Madeira. Whereon the Portuguese Government immediately complied, and their Nyasaland expedition was withdrawn, to the gratification of all Britons there.

There was further serious trouble involving the suspension of the river navigation in February 1884, this time caused by the action of a trader, Fenwick, in the Makololo district. Originally he came to the country as a carpenter in the Blantyre Mission, and on his discharge was given work for a time by the African Lakes Company. Thereafter he started business as a trader on his own account. Practically the only available paying export was ivory. Knowing that the Company refused to trade in spirits, and that many of the chiefs desired to procure Portuguese rum, he expected to make a good thing out of a combined traffic of rum and ivory.

On going down the Shire on his way to the coast, he accepted a tusk from Chipatula to be sold for him in Quilimane. On his return with a cargo of goods, including a quantity of trade rum, the chief was dissatisfied with the return Fenwick offered him for the sale of the tusk, and several heated altercations ensued. After one of these, as Chipatula was leaving, Fenwick, who was a man of hot temper, shot him dead. Immediately he called out to the natives, "I have shot Chipatula, but will myself be your chief". Their answer was to seize their guns and fire at him. He pushed off in his boat pursued by many shots and took refuge on an island below the confluence of the Shire and Ruo only a few hundred yards from the scene of the murder. He was a good shot, and there, firing from the cover of the reeds, he held the natives at bay. But when coming down to the river to drink, a native sniper from the other bank killed him. His head was cut off, and put on a pole in the village.

Chipatula's heir, Chikusi, a lad of about twenty, sent a letter in English to Mandala demanding delivery of Mrs. Fenwick and her children and trade goods of various kinds to a very considerable amount. The latter tribute to be repeated after six months. But already, by mysterious native 'telegraphy', news had come that Chikusi was preparing an expedition. On this news the double-storied house at Mandala was strongly fortified.

When the messenger arrived with his note, he was taken to the centre upper room where all available guns, duly cleaned and prepared, stood thickly round the walls. The letter was read over aloud and then torn into small pieces before his eyes, and he was informed that the demand for Mrs. Fenwick and her children could not be entertained. He was reminded that Chipatula knew well that Fenwick had for some time past no connection with the Company, arid that the Company was in no way responsible for his crime.

Strict watch was kept, and a message was sent overland to the captain and engineer of the *Lady Nyasa* on no account to proceed beyond Mpatsa's, below the Makololo country. The letter duly reached the captain, but later, a communication, written in English from Chikusi, enticed him to Chiromo, where the steamer was seized. He was stripped almost naked, but allowed to leave on foot. After several days painful journey he arrived at Mandala, suffering from dysentery. Not only the goods aboard but all brasswork and copper piping about the boiler and engines were looted, and the steamer was allowed to sink, fortunately on a shallow hank.

Captain Foote, R.N., who had recently been appointed British Consul, and Mr. Rankin, his assistant, accompanied by the Company's chief engineer, Fred Morrison, set off to interview Ramakukan, the paramount Makololo chief and along with him, proceeded to Chiromo. John Moir remained at Mandala to be ready to defend the small British community in case of attack.

While Consul Foote and Ramakukan were conducting protracted negotiations with Chikusi, Morrison and his men visited the steamer and floated her. The main demand that Mrs. Fenwick the children should be given up was successfully resisted, but further goods, in addition to those already looted from the fully-laden steamer, were promised, and eventually handed over by the Company which in these early days often paid for the misdeeds of others. Even this arrangement was only agreed to with great reluctance, and the party was glad to get away by the steamer, which had been cleverly repaired, in a makeshift manner, by Morrison.

During the time the river was closed, considerable shortage of goods and provisions was experienced; and overland convoys carrying mails and goods to and from Quilimane were arranged, passing far to the east of the Makololo territory.

# CHAPTER XXI

### THE SLAVE TRADERS ATTACK US

Karonga, at the Lake Nyasa end of the Stevenson Road, developed into an important station. It had no harbour where the steamer could lie in safety, but in calm weather she could approach the beach, and cargo was then quickly loaded and discharged in boats. In bad weather or during the season when sudden squalls might be expected, she could shelter in the Kambwe Lagoon, two miles to the north. There, crossing a sandbar, she was in complete shelter behind a sandspit.

A good house was erected not far from Karonga beach, near a circle of large, handsome Misiunguti trees which were held in reverence by the natives. As it was the terminus of the Stevenson Road, cross-country traffic was dispatched from the station, and Tanganyika and western Arabs were drawn to it as a market for their ivory.

We placed one of our best agents in the station, L. Monteith Fotheringham, who became a power in the district, attracting and becoming friendly with a large number of Arabs and natives. Trade increased and a considerable quantity of ivory was secured. As it was shipped by steamer, the slaves who would have been captured to carry it by caravan to the coast escaped for the time being.

Gradually Arabs became frequent visitors, and for the most part appeared friendly. At the same time they disliked the British because of the check put on the slave trade. No slave raids were allowed to be carried out against our Karonga villagers, while in the populous districts at the north end, the Wankonde chiefs and warriors with their spears and shields had till then been able to overcome any marauding Arabs. No doubt the increasingly stringent measures adopted by the British Navy against slaving operations on the Zanzibar coast, and the exploitation of their Manyema slave preserves on the Congo by explorers and embryo governments, also disconcerted them considerably. They determined, therefore, to strike their hardest on Lake Nyasa, where there were no defensive forces and by a combined attack on the Wankonde, break their power and expose that populous district to their slave raids.

About 1886, some Arabs received permission from a small independent chief some twelve miles west of Karonga, near the Stevenson Road, to build a hut beside the Rukuru River. Then, still under the guise of friendship, they erected a stockade, and became so strong as to be able to impose their will on the natives. They proceeded to build two strong villages at Msalemu and at Kopakopas on both sides of the road close to the Rukuru ford, about five miles from Karonga.

By killing two native chiefs, Kasote and Mwinimtete, in July 1887, they raised trouble with the natives, and in retaliation destroyed the native villages. Forays followed on both sides. The Arabs still professed friendship to the British and Fotheringham's influence was able to postpone a general outbreak of hostilities. The natives retired northwards, but in October the Arabs, by means of a messenger who claimed to have come from Fotheringham, induced them to come south to Karonga for a conference.

When encamped in the reedy swamps bordering the Kambwe Lagoon, they were ambushed by the Arabs, who surrounded them and set fire to the tall bango reeds and grass which were highly inflammable at that time of year. The native warriors charged into the open with their spears, only to be shot down by the Arab gunners. As the fierce fires approached, the unfortunate men, women, and children were forced either to seek death in the mud and water of the lagoon, swarming with crocodiles, or to yield themselves up to the tender mercies of the bloodthirsty ruga-ruga, to be maltreated and shot, or to be seized as slaves, as chance or fancy dictated. Mlozi, the self-appointed Sultan and his Arab headmen, were seated in trees at points of vantage watching the proceedings.

Having destroyed the native villages, the Arabs sent a defiant message to the British at Karonga. The Company's policy having been to extend voluntary trading by peaceful means, we had no standing army or police force. Located at our station were only Fotheringham and his assistant, Nicoll, with eight trustworthy natives. Beyond a dozen muzzle-loading trade rifles, there were only thirty-two Sniders and Chassepot breech-loaders, and for them only 1330 cartridges.

Fortunately, on 4th November 1887, our small steamer *Ilala* arrived, with Consul O'Neill of Mozambique, Mr. (later Sir) Alfred Sharpe1, Rev. L. Scott, and Dr. Tomory. As the store buildings could be cut off from the water supply, a stockade was constructed between the buildings and the Lake, with walls about four feet high, as well as an annexe to shelter our villagers. The station goods and provisions were then carried into the stockade. When the Arabs in overwhelming numbers called on the British to surrender, they met with a prompt and definite refusal. Consul O'Neill, who had had valuable experience of slavers in the Royal Navy, undertook to organise the defence. Tents and native huts were erected, and the stockade strengthened.

On Wednesday, 23rd November, the Arabs attacked and were repulsed. Nicoll was at once sent north to my old friends Mwakyusa and Manjiwara to call for the assistance of their native warriors.

Next day, at 5 a.m. the Arabs renewed the assault in full force, with five hundred gunners and innumerable spearsmen. They came on from different directions, subjecting the besiegers to a nasty cross-fire. Sheltering in and behind Karonga House and bricksheds they pressed the attack. The defenders waited until they were well within range and met them with such hot and steady fire that they had to retire. Instead of fortifying the bricksheds they burned them down, to the great relief of the besieged. A sortie organised by the Consul and Mr Sharpe succeeded in burning two of the houses, but failed to ignite the store.

Then the Arabs endeavoured by regular siege to reduce the station. They made a heavy wooden fence on the roof of the store, eighty yards distant, and erected five shooting platforms protected by heavy logs in a large tree one hundred yards off. From these points their sharpshooters for some days kept up a steady and galling fire.

The defenders made deep trenches in the sand, in which they could move from one part of the defences to the other without exposing themselves, and large pits in which they took up their quarters. The tents, left to attract the Arab fire, were riddled with their bullets. As ammunition was so scanty, only the best shots were allowed to fire. Mr. Sharpe, with his elephant rifle, sent a bullet through the heavy wooden door of the store to the great amazement of the Arabs, scattering those sheltered there. The attack was kept up from all directions, but watchfulness and resource foiled the enemy at every point.

As the store with its fortifications, only eighty yards off; particularly menaced the besieged, two Mambwe capitaos were asked to go and fire it. Crawling under a bank and through the grass, they managed, very pluckily, to get behind it, though it was occupied by the Arabs, then putting a firestick into the thatch they succeeded in regaining our stockade. An hour later the fire burst out, and the building anddefences were destroyed.

Four days and five nights the little band of defenders held off every attack, and on Monday morning, 28th November, after an exceptionally heavy fusillade, the firing ceased. At first it was thought they were trying to lure the defenders into the open, but it was found they were gone, and all hands began to demolish their defences.

Then Nicoll arrived with five thousand of the northenders, and the siege was over. With the aid of these Wamwamba, Mirambo's village was assailed, but it was found evacuated, and was destroyed. Preparations were made to attack Msalemus, but the Wamwamba would not wait, and as our own natives were averse to a further occupation of our stockade, the party went north to the Nsessi River and encamped.

On the 9th of December the *Ilala* returned, bringing Consul Hawes from Blantyre, John Moir, and two others. She went off again at once to collect all available ammunition. The Wamwamba again responded to our call, and on 23rd of December a large party started for Miozi's stockade, which was charged and entered and the houses destroyed one by one as they proceeded. But as soon as our native volunteers could lay hands on a tusk, a cow, or truss of calico, they decamped at once with their spoil and our ranks grew thinner and thinner, until my brother, who was attacking on the left flank, found himself with only two or three white companions and a dozen Mandala natives, with more than half of the village still in the hands of the enemy. Then he fell, shot at short range through the thigh, the bullet fortunately not damaging the main artery or bone. In his fall his spectacles were knocked off and he was practically blind. Fortunately he recovered them unbroken, and was assisted to the rear. The attack, after having inflicted heavy loss on our enemies, both in men and goods, was abandoned, and our forces returned to the Nsessi camp.

The rainy season now being on, most of the Europeans went south, but Fotheringham and four others, in order to protect the natives from the vengeance of the Arabs, proceeded to Mwiniwandas, sixty-five miles up the Stevenson Road, and kept the Arabs in check.

Meanwhile news of what was happening reached Glasgow, and in January 1888 a meeting of those interested in Africa was convened. Our Secretary, Mr. Ewing, did yeoman service in interesting the Foreign Office and the British public in our antislavery campaign. The different Scottish Churches whose African missions were threatened, also the Rev. Horace Wailer, editor of Livingstone's Last Journals - a Church of England clergyman, formerly a member of the Universities Mission, who had accompanied Dr. Livingstone to the Shire Highlands, and Professor Henry Drummond, who at the request of our Company had gone to Lake Nyasa and beyond Karonga, all combined to assist the Directors of the Company in calling the attention of the British Government to what was happening.

We pointed out that the country had been discovered by Dr. Livingstone, was then occupied only by British Missionary Societies, and by our Company, which at its own risk and cost was engaged in a desperate struggle in defending the British and the native inhabitants from hordes of Arab immigrant slavers. Lord Salisbury was sympathetic, and approved of the permanent occupation of the country between Nyasa and Tanganyika by the Company for the protection of the people.

In August a committee was formed of those interested, to control hostilities and direct affairs at the north end. Arms and ammunition were purchased and dispatched. It is interesting to know that, although the Portuguese on the coast were aware that the white community on Lake Nyasa was fighting for its existence against the slavers, at great risk, they, on the strength of some anti-slavery regulations, detained these same British supplies in the Quilimane custom-house. It was only after much delay that word of this could reach London, and diplomatic pressure on Lisbon removed the obstruction. Immediate delivery of these arms might have made a great difference in the progress of the campaign.

Notes:

1. Sir Alfred Sharpe (1853 - 1935) started a Foreign Service career as a magistrate in Fiji from 1885 - 1887. After his involvement in the anti-slave ars he became Vice-Consul in Nyasaland in 1891. Moving on he was appointed the Acting Commissioner for British Central Africa in 1894, before taking up the post of Commissioner and Consul General in 1897. He finished his career in Africa in 1907 by being appointed Governor of Nyasaland.

# CHAPTER XXII

**WOUNDED**

In Nyasaland the struggle proceeded. On the return of Consul Hawes to Blantyre from the scene of operations he counselled the abandonment of the country on the ground of our lack of force to withstand the Arabs, and he did all he could to prevent our return north. As this would have meant the annihilation of our native allies, and the withdrawal of the

Livingstonia Mission and probably of others farther south, we felt that his advice could not be taken. Every available member of our staff volunteered to assist, with the approval of practically the entire community, and we prepared for a new expedition against the enemy under my leadership. Five of our Company men were chosen, and we were able to raise sixty Mandala natives and one hundred guns, 200 lb. of powder, and a supply of cartridges.

Mr. Buchanan, the planter, who acted as British Vice-Consul when Mr. Hawes retired, accompanied us as a non-combatant and as a British official, to try in the first place methods of conciliation. He came in the Universities Mission steamer, *Charles Jansen*, and got into touch with the Arab headman. Hopes were entertained of a settlement, as they admitted that their attack on the whites had been unprovoked and agreed to destroy their stockades and leave the country within two months. Mr. Buchanan said he would carry their proposals to Karonga, which we had reoccupied. The Arab chiefs arranged to meet the Consul and myself next day. We went and waited till nightfall, but none put in an appearance. A message was therefore sent to MIozi that as he had broken off negotiations the truce would come to an end. A defiant reply was received. Mr. Buchanan could do no more. He issued a proclamation, in Arabic, to all loyal subjects of the Sultan of Zanzibar, to withold support from Miozi and his followers, and then returned south.

On our reoccupying Karonga we found that the station and stockade had been destroyed, and that hundreds of square miles of fertile country were relapsing into wilderness. We rebuilt the stockade to enclose our tents and grass huts, and kept up a watch day and night against attack. Sentries were posted to the south, west, and north, and the European on guard made three rounds during his night watch. It took about half an hour to make each eerie round. The tall grass and bushes hung thick with dew or rain, hyenas and snakes were about, and at any thicket Arabs might be lurking.

Fotheringham and I started at 2 a.m. on the 28th to reconnoitre the enemy's position five miles off. Crossing the Rukuru, we proceeded in soaking rain by a long roundabout way till we were opposite the stockades. These were double, of strong poles ten or twelve feet high, and between the walls earth and clay were pounded six or seven feet high to make the whole bulletproof. Loopholes were mad for gun fire. Near the principal gate and corners were high 'crow's nests,' defended by heavy planks, loopholed for sharpshooters. Outside the stockade was a deep ditch filled with thorns and sharpened stakes.

Under cover of darkness and pelting rain we passed close to the walls, first of Mlozi's, and then of Msalemus' stockade, about half a mile off on the other side of the Stevenson Road. The thatched huts were crowded down close to the stockades. It struck me that if we could set them on fire the Arabs would be forced to abandon the loopholes. Then we could charge up to the walls, get our rifles through their loopholes, and defend ourselves till we could make a breach. After that it would be man to man and gun to gun.

I soon designed a fire-dart to be shot from a 12-bore muzzle-loading rifle. It was made of solid bamboo about twelve inches long. Just behind its point, a hole was bored through it, and from the ends of this, deep spirals to steady its flight were cut down to the base. Through the hole and down the spirals were inserted bark cloth, which protruded for a foot or so beyond the dart. Damp gunpowder was rubbed into the cloth, dried at the end of the tails, so as to make sure that it would take fire on discharge. To prevent the gun bursting, trade powder was winnowed till only the largest grains remained. Their slow combustion minimised the danger of an explosion, and I soon found myself able to fire about 150 yards with very good direction.

At this stage, Mr. Nicoll and Dr. Cross of the Livingstonia Mission arrived from Mwiniwandas. On 10th April all preparations possible in the circumstances were complete, and at 6 a.m. we started, a party of eight white men and nearly five hundred natives, with 270 guns or rifles. With me were Fotheringham, Lindsay, Peebles, Nicoll, T. Morrison, Bell, and Dr. Cross. The two last mentioned were in charge of reserve ammunition and the ambulance department.

After firing three revolver shots to warn any friendly Arabs to retire, we advanced and discharged some volleys with long range rifles at four hundred or five hundred yards. As we got nearer we sent some elephant bullets from our heavy rifles through the crow's-nest watch towers, and soon emptied them. The besieged replied vigorously, but shot wildly. I got up to a large ant-hill about one hundred yards from the village, and settled down to the fire-dart gun. After half a dozen shots I had the satisfaction of seeing the huts take fire in more than one place, and, as arranged, the charge began.

Victory seemed within our grasp when Msalemu and his men made a sortie from his village half a mile away, firing hard against our flanks. This so alarmed our north-end natives that they scattered and ran, but Fotheringham, with twenty of his station boys, boldly attacked the newcomers and drove them back. It took half an hour to rally our natives, but by that time the flames in the burning houses were less fierce, and the bulletproof stockades were again manned by the defenders.

Loth to desist when victory had been so near, we rallied for a last charge. In the face of a hail of bullets we made some advance, when I was struck by a shot that shattered my right arm just above the elbow. I was carried on the back of a trusty native to the doctor's tree, where first-aid was skilfully rendered by Dr. Cross. Unable to reach the stockade, we withdrew the attack and retired on Karonga. The Arabs tried to molest our party, but in the open they did not dare to approach.

My arm was so shattered and swollen that immediate amputation was recommended. I suggested two days delay, and by that time the improvement was so marked that it seemed possible to save it. Nursed by Dr. Cross, I left for the south in the '*Ilala*' on 27th April, while Fotheringham, who remained in charge, harassed the Arabs whenever they left the shelter of their stockades, until further reinforcements could be sent up to him from the south.

After two days tossing in the little steamer, I reached Bandawe, then the headquarters of the Livingstonia Mission, where I was hospitably received by Dr. and Mrs. Laws. The doctor gave considerable encouragement and fashioned a metal rest, which greatly eased the arm during the further rough travelling. I was able to hang this arm-rest to the roof of the cabin, and on the long machila run of thirty-five miles from Matope to Mandala, I swung it from the machila-pole, which minimised the discomfort of the journey. The native machilamen did their best to carry their burden gently, I was no light-weight, and only rested on the long road three or four times. When nearing our destination, Blantyre and Mandala volunteers rushed up to assist the tired carriers, and late that night I was laid down at Mandala House to be nursed by my wife, who had only heard of my being wounded that morning. As fever supervened, I was ordered home by first boat. No native woman would, at that time, venture to go so far as England, so a small boy was engaged as nurse to our baby daughter, and we were carried down to the steamer, sailed via the Zambesi and Kwakwa to Quilimane, and thence home. The wound was daily washed through with antiseptics until our arrival in Scotland.

In Edinburgh several leading physicians and surgeons vied in their kind attention and advice. To obviate a rigid elbow, Professor Annandale made a skilful excision of the elbow-joint. The fingers, grown stiff, were bent under chloroform, and then massaged until restored to some degree of usefulness. It was a matter for great thankfulness that my arm, though crippled, was saved. It has since been, and is, of very considerable use.

My recovery from such a serious wound, notwithstanding the primitive accommodation in our stockade, and the long, slow, and painful journey to the coast, I consider a proof, if that were necessary, of the great value to health of total abstinence and clean living under the most trying climatic conditions.

By August 1888 I was able to meet the Company's Directors in Glasgow, and it was agreed to form the Nyasa Anti-Slavery and Defence Fund. To enable our combatants to overcome the resistance of the Arab stockades, we purchased and dispatched a 7-pound muzzle-loading Armstrong gun and ammunition. We gained approval from the Foreign Office, who made representations to Lisbon in order to avoid customs delay.

# CHAPTER XXIII

### HOW THE WAR ENDED

Meantime at Karonga, Fotheringham gave the Arabs no peace, harassing them when they left their stockades, and on several occasions freeing slaves whom they captured.

From Mandala my brother requested our Natal agents to engage volunteers and secure guns and ammunition. Hearing that a Captain Lugard, D.S.O.,[1] was near the coast on his way to South Africa, our community invited him to come and render assistance, which he was good enough to do. He was requested to take charge of the operations, the Company rendering him all the assistance in its power.

Before the end of May, John Moir had sufficiently recovered from his wound to be able to go north with a new expedition. It comprised Captain Lugard (in command), Smith, Stewart, Watson, Nisbet, and Moore from the Company's service, and nine men engaged in Natal. There were now twenty-four white men, also Mandala and Atonga natives. Military discipline was introduced with regular drills.

On 1st June Captain Lugard and Fotheringham reconnoitred by night, and on the 15th a big attack was made. Lugard divided his force into seven companies, under charge of my brother, Fotheringham, Lindsay, Smith,

Peebles, Morrison, and Nicoll, to whom were assigned definite positions in the attack. they marched by night and the assaults began at daybreak. In face of a heavy fusillade several parties reached the stockade and fired through the loopholes into the village. But the stockade of heavy trees, bulletproof below, interlaced high up with thorns and creepers, proved to strong to break through. Captain Lugard pluckily endeavoured to tear down the upper part, but was shot, the bullet breaking his left arm after passing through his right and tearing across his breast. Between nine and ten o'clock it became evident that the stockade was too strong for the resources at our command, and an orderly retreat was made. We had attempted the impossible, and failed. One South African and eight of our natives were killed, and many were wounded. The Arabs doubtless lost heavily.

For more than three months the indomitable Fotheringham held the fort, sending out bands, sometimes under white men, sometimes composed of Atonga or station boys only, intercepting supplies, releasing slaves, and assisting friendly villages.

On 25th October Captain Lugard and my brother returned to Karonga, but pending the arrival of the 7-pounder Armstrong gun, the former went out hunting. Fotheringham remained in charge. When on the look-out for game, Captain Lugard descried an Arab dhow with supplies approaching Deep Bay from the other aide of the Lake. The Arabs tried to land, but Captain Lugard attacked them. After a sharp fight the enemy had to retreat with many killed and wounded, and a leaking boat. By baling they managed to re-cross the Lake to their starting-point, and there the dhow foundered.

Early in 1889 the long-looked-for gun arrived, and another assault under Captain Lugard was planned for 21st February. Lieutenant Crawshay, who had come back to the country for game-shooting, also joined the party.

Mr. Sharpe had been sent the previous day farther inland to prevent the arrival of enemy reinforcements. The various companies took their assigned stations, and Lieutenant Crawshay, assisted by Nisbet and Auld, brought up the gun, which was placed on a hill about one thousand yards distant from the stockades. It was well served. The shells, bursting inside the village, destroyed houses and killed many Arabs, but did not make a breach in the stockade through which an assault could be carried home. After three hours shelling the party retired. It was decided to await large attacking forces from the north-end to take the stockade by assault with the aid of the gun. Owing to wet weather and flooded rivers only eight hundred came, and on 14th March the stockades were again shelled, but not destroyed.[2]

Next day the steamer left with Captain Lugard, Sharpe, Crawshay, Burton and Hector, leaving only six fighting Europeans along with Dr. Cross, who accompanied the expeditions and rendered much valuable help as medical attendant.

On the 18th March another gun attack was made. But it was considered better to adopt waiting and harassing tactics until more assistance could be procured. Later, a fortified station was opened at Deep Bay in order to prevent supplies reaching the Arabs from the coast. This was in charge of Lieutenant Crawshay, who had returned to assist us.

The dreary struggle went on until at length the steamer,

arriving on 20th September, brought news that Mr. (later Sir) H. H. Johnston,[3] British Consul at Mozambique, was coming to open negotiations with the Arabs. He had with him an envoy from the Sultan of Zanzibar and a headman of Jumbe of Kota Kota. A truce was therefore arranged.

On 15th October Mr. Johnston arrived, and got into touch with Mlozi through Jumbe's headman, and a meeting was arranged to take place half-way to the stockade.

The Arabs expressed their desire to make peace, but they wanted runaway women returned. This the Consul saw was not practicable, and refused. He placed in their hands his terms of peace, and these they accepted.

On 22nd October 1889, Consul Johnston, Fotheringham, and Dr. Cross, with two others, met the Arabs, and the treaty to restore peace was signed with due formalities and rejoicing. The terms were:

1. The north-end natives were to be allowed toreturn to their homes in peace.

2. They were not to be molested afterwards by the Arabs.

3. No new Arab villages were to be built north of the Rukurn or within three miles of our road.

4. The stockaded villages were to be removedfrom the road.

5. The Company would hold themselves responsible for the behaviour of their native allies

6. Any hostile act against natives would be interpreted by the Company as hostile to itself

Everything we had fought for was thus conceded, and soon the Arabs paid a visit to our station, and spears were broken by various native chiefs to symbolise the end of hostilities. It was significant that some of the principal Arabs, usually well clad, were in rags. They were short of food and hard up for cloth.

So, after two years and three months, ended the Karonga War, a small but historic fight for freedom, conducted largely by the volunteer staff of the African Lakes Company and almost entirely at that Company's expense. Valuable assistance was rendered by Consul O'Neill, Mr. (now Sir) Alfred Sharpe, Captain (now General) Sir Francis Lugard, Lieutenant Crawshay, and Consul (now Sir) H. H. Johnston, as Government officials and volunteers not connected with the Company, and their services are gratefully acknowledged, but the leading spirit who saw it through from start to finish was L. Monteith Fotheringham, to whom the Company and Nyasaland owe profound gratitude. On my brother's return to Scotland, Fotheringham was appointed African manager of the Company, a position he filled with credit. His death at Chinde, in 1895, when returning to this country on his second furlough, was deeply mourned.

The Arabs kept the terms of the treaty for several years, but in 1895, after the British Government had taken over the country as a British Protectorate, Mlozi revolted, insulted a Government messenger, and defied the Governor. A military expedition under British officers, Indian non-coms., and drilled native troops, attacked what was believed by the

Arabs to be an impregnable stockade. After heavy fighting the stockade was taken, and Miozi was found hiding in a cellar. He was duly tried and hanged, and so ended the slaver's power at the north end of the lake.

---

Notes

1 A book could almost be written about our Captain Lugard alone. He went to India from England, as a captain in the British Army, having fallen in love with a divorcee back home. On hearing that his beloved had had a serious accident, he returned home post haste. He was devastated, when on arrival at her house he found her in the arms of another admirer.

Heartbroken, he immediately left the Army and sailed for Zanzibar, reputedly looking for a cause to devote himself and thereby forget his lost love. On arrival at Zanzibar he heard tell of the plight of the Africa Lakes Company in a fight with the Arab slave traders and their African allies. He left immediately for Blantyre to offer his services.

Following the cessation of hostilities, Lugard travelled North joining up with Mackinnon's Imperial East Africa Company and helped in the opening up of Uganda to British Influence.

2. This 7 - pounder gun, used so effectively in the Arab Slave wars, was preserved and now holds pride of place in the boardroom of the African Lakes headquarters in Blantyre.

3. Sir H. H. Johnson (1858 - 1927) was actually an acclaimed Zoologist and painter. He led the scientific expeditions to Portuguese West Africa (Angola) and on to Mount Kilamanjaro. In 1885 he was appointed Vice Consul to the Cameroons and then Consul to the Niger Coast Protectorate. In 1888 he was made Consul for Mozambique and from 1889 - 1891 he was Consul General for newly formed British Central Africa. He finished his Foreign Service career as the Consul General for Uganda.

A prolific author, he wrote books and reports on subjects as varied as ' A History of the Colonisation of Africa by Alien Races 1899 - 1913' to 'The Black Man's Part in the War 1917'.

# CHAPTER XXIV

### TRADING SCENES IN UJIJI

In order to make a further advance northwards to promote trade, make arrangements with chiefs and secure treaties which would be handed over to the British Government should the latter consider it advisable to extend its protection to them. I, along with Mrs. Moir, started from Mandala for Tanganyika in May 1890. We had a large stock of trade goods and a few Mandala boys to act as guards and personal servants.

Our route lay thirty-five miles overland to Matope, which still had sufficient water to enable the *Domira* to reach it regularly. Two days steaming took us to Lake Nyasa. We called at Cape Maclear, the original Livingstonia Mission Station, and then met with various native chiefs, including the Arab Jumbe of Kota Kota, making arrangements for acquiring from him mineral rights. We finally reached Karonga after a voyage, including stoppages, of nine and a half days. While awaiting a call from MIozi, our chief opponent in the Arab war, we crossed the Lake to Parambira Bay, where we had a station, having bought land from the chief. Later this bay, at the foot of the steep Livingstone Mountains with deep water close in-shore, was in the course of European diplomacy, passed over to the Germans, who called it Old Langenberg.

Next day, Mlozi, who was still on his best behaviour, arrived with his warriors, a villainous-looking crowd. We exchanged salutations, and he promised to stick to his bargain made by the treaty. Inside our Karonga stockade, with our 7-pounder gun as a background, he and his men stood for a photo, a peaceful camera shot at the man who had shattered my right arm.

At Karonga we recommenced our overland march to Tanganyika, a journey of twenty days. We tried to 'break in' two of the common Unyamwezi donkeys for riding and succeeded, but their funereal walking pace was too slow for the carriers and when we made them trot or gallop they scattered the porters from the narrow path. They were taken over the Rukuru River by the brute force of many carriers. At night extra defences had to be erected to keep off lions and hyenas. So, after a day or two, we sent the animals back, having found them useless, and set out to tramp the long journey of two hundred and twenty miles.

When we reached the hills, the Stevenson Road saved us many a difficult scramble, but at the unfinished portion there were many bits of rough climbing, specially trying to the bare feet of the carriers where the surface was covered with loose sharp quartz. The knowing ones provided themselves with sandals of game-hide.

At this point I quote from a letter which my wife wrote home to a friend when half-way across the plateau:

"I will tell you how we spend our time. Suppose we have got over the first day of toiling up rocky hills, on a rough, uneven footpath, every step an effort, and hour after hour of tramp, tramp, dragging wearily past; suppose we are fairly on to the cool, high plateau and our legs in first-class condition for marching, here is how we do. 5 a.m. - Sound asleep, heaped with blankets, for it is very cold at night. 5.15am -We begin to waken and call out, "Dojimi, is the sky beginning to redden?" Dojimi calls back, "Very, very little "; then we say, "Make the tea," and forthwith proceed to crawl out of our warm bed and with all haste get into our half-damp clothes - no time for washing or hairdressing, and with perhaps a blanket on for a bit, open the tent door and go out into the chilly, cold grey light of the first dawn.

We find our two canvas chairs and little table set, and a fine wood fire to warm us, and tea and scones all ready, and while we drink our tea the camp becomes very lively. The men all get to their loads, those in charge of the tent take it down and roll it up, others fold the beds, others put the pots and pans, and cups and biscuits, into the big baskets they are carried in.

Before six o'clock the whole sixty-one of us are ready to set out, all shivering and cold. Then we get up a shout, and all the carriers call out, "Ulendo, Ulendo, Ulendo, Ku Tanganyika," and all down the line we hear "Ulendo, Ulendo." This simply means, "March, march, let us march for Tanganyika," and they get as cheery as possible with shouting, and forget about their heavy loads, and the thick, cold dew. We usually make some of the carriers go on before so as to shake off some of this dew, which sometimes is very wetting. As a rule we are pretty well soaked in the course of half an hour, and go along in a sort of shrivelled-up state, creepy and cold, till the glorious sun rises over the horizon, immediately we feel warm, and the whole caravan marches along single file, quickly and happily.

Very soon Fred and I get to the front, as the carriers stop often to rest, and on we go, march, march, trudge, trudge, step by step, over that knoll, and across this stream, past a grassy plain, and through a long stretch of forest, on and on, a drink of water at one place, and ten minutes rest at another, till we have gone perhaps ten or twelve miles, and reach the camp or village where we intend to stop and have breakfast- this usually between nine and ten o'clock. I have found out it is so easy to say we are going to walk to Tanganyika and back - a distance of only 480 miles, but how different it is when it comes to one mile after another, to walk along sturdily for twenty minutes and remember at the end we have only made one mile! One has plenty of time for thought, and I find myself composing endless letters, and thinking of what I would like to write to each of the dear people at home.

Fred spends his time hunting for gold. He walks along with an iron crow-bar, and breaks off pieces of rock and stones, and gets specimens out of all the burns and watercourses. These he grinds in a mortar and washes, but so far we have found no gold.

Well, to get on with the day. About ten o'clock we reach the village, very tired, hungry, and meltingly hot, for by this time the sun is high above us. We fix on a shady spot, and our boys go off and get firewood and water. In a very short time the rice pot is boiling away, and the stew is simmering. In the meantime the very primitive inhabitants come out of their stockaded village to stare at the white people, and presently they hear that the second white man is a woman, a fact which astonishes them very much, and the women and children now venture near and gaze at the creature who is said to be a woman, but who to their eyes is so little like one.

The reason is that I wear a belt, and have, unfortunately for the credit of Englishwomen here, a waist. This is what puzzles them. She has no stomach; how can she be so thin if she is a woman? Yet they say she is Chindevu's wife, so English women must be like her. I explain that if the black women were dressed in my clothes, they would be just the same, but it is no use, and I feel quite disappointed with myself and if it weren't for fear of sunstrokes and other difficulties, I would like very much to dress in a big bath towel, and then probably I would be much admired. As it is, Fred gets all the admiration; they think his beard magnificent.

Feeling so unworthy of my sex, I do not very much enjoy the staring process, and at first was a good deal overcome by the terribly nude condition of the people. The men are very much dressed in a small skin, and many simply have a bit of bark string tied round the waist, and a few leaves slung on in front. The ladies here wear a loose string of beads or shells round their bodies, and a piece of bark cloth or calico, if they have it, fastened to this in front, brought up between the limbs and spread out behind. They have some strings of beads round their necks, and brass bracelets and anklets. Every one without exception during this cold season is frightfully dirty, and covered with dust. How would you enjoy a crowd of these ladies, some fat and young, some old and shrivelled, some with big babies, some with little, all in the national costume, to come and curiously look at and talk about the white man and his queer-looking wife! We usually get presented with a goat or a fowl, and some native flour, and then we give the chief two yards or so of calico, and he begs for a lick of salt, or a needle into the bargain; then we have breakfast, and sometimes I make scones or pancakes.

Usually we set out again about two o'clock, and walk till four or five, but we cannot go so far as we often wish, as many of the carriers have heavy loads, over 60 lb. calico, and get tired travelling long distances, day after day. As soon as we get to camp, the tent is pitched, and the carriers settle down round it, in groups of men from different tribes. The first care of every one is to get firewood, for they keep up blazing fires all night, both for warmth and also to frighten away wild beasts. They usually have from fourteen to twenty splendid fires, and we have a big one to ourselves, which is most comforting. The finest time of all the day is now, when we are resting beside the camp-fire. Every one is happy and cheery, talking and laughing, and you have no idea what a pretty sight it is. The calm sky and stars overhead, the trees, and fires, and black figures round them, and the porridge pots! I can't tell you how nice it is, and can only hope that some day you may see it yourself.

We turn in about eight o'clock, and know little more till next morning. We have a loaded revolver at hand in case a hyena should want to investigate matters in the tent!"

Half-way across, near a small but reputedly perennial stream, we fixed on a site for a new station - Mwenzo or Fife.

When we camped near villages, from the natives came the constant and urgent cry of "Wawemba!" They feared the forays of these dreaded warriors and their villages were strongly stockaded or built in positions as inaccessible as possible. They gladly signed a petition asking for the protection of the British.

When we reached the Saisi River, we found it flooded, but we made a framework of tent poles and deck chairs, on which, carried on the shoulders of a dozen strong natives, we managed to get over without mishap. This was not so simple as it seems. The river, usually confined to a deep channel, six to eight feet wide, was at this time, owing to high floods, a great stretch of water, one hundred yards from bank to bank. In ordinary times the channel was bridged by two or three trees thrown across. These were now deeply submerged, and our carriers, shoulder deep, had to feel their way along the branches, holding us on the frame-work above their heads, one, then another, would lose his footing and disappear in the water, but between them, after many hours work, they got us and all the loads safely over.

We next climbed the Fwambo hills and reached the London Missionary Society's station, where we were kindly entertained for a night.

Then we passed on to what had, on my previous journey, been the pretty little lake of Chila. Looking down on it we saw a distinct mirage of blue, rippling water. When we reached it there was not a drop of water but only dry, soft, light sand into which our feet sank deep. It is probable that some of the frequent earthquakes of the region had cracked the wall of rock across the mouth of the valley which formed the Lake. In some way the rift must again have been closed, as in later years it once more became, and still remains, a lake.

Twelve miles descent of a hillside infested with tse-tse fly, and at last the blue water of Tanganyika lay before us. Soon we received a welcome from J.L. Nicoll, late assistant at Karonga, then busily engaged in building our station at Kituta.

Our journey north to Ujiji, thanks to the kindness of Capt. A. I. Swann of the London Missionary Society, was performed in the Mission boat, *Morning Star*. Their steamer, *Good News*, my old friend which we had wrestled with on her journey to Lake Tanganyika, was then sunk at her moorings, but later, I am glad to say, she was floated again.

On the third day out, we touched at Karema, one of the many stations of the White Fathers of Cardinal Lavigerie's Mission. One of their plans was to secure children, many of them by purchase, whom they hoped to rear without any knowledge of their native superstitions. They were very hospitable, and sent us on our way with pleasant recollections.

We reached Ujiji in five days. Famous as the spot where Stanley found Livingstone, it was then an important interior town. Here we were hospitably received by Rumaliza (Mahomet bin Khalfan), the Governor, who regaled us with strong coffee in small cups, supplemented by Huntley & Palmer's honey-wafer biscuits, fresh from a tin carried all the way from Zanzibar. He gave us a large room in his own house near his harem, and assigned to us a cook and plenty 'girl-boys' (girl servants) to wait on us, so as to obviate the attendance of our lads in his establishment.

There was a large native village near the open landing-place, somewhat protected from north and south gales, but good shelter for a steamer could only be had at Kigoma, a mile or two to the north, now the terminus of the Dar-es-Salam Tanganyika Railway constructed by the Germans. Several Arab establishments lay in different directions outside Ujiji. They were usually oblong, with high stone walls, in the centre of the narrow end of which was a heavy wooden gate. As one entered into the large square court the main house stood opposite, occupying the whole width. About the centre was the main door behind a veranda, and beyond that a reception room. Behind the house was a smaller court with the women's apartments and cooking arrangements. Round the main court were stores and open sheds where interviews took place with other Arabs or native chiefs and headmen. In case of trouble, warriors walking on the roofs of these buildings could defend the 'Tembe' sheltered by the top of the wall.

The room allotted to us was large, forty by fifteen feet, and in a corner we set up our camp table and chairs. The only furniture consisted of two Arab bedsteads and mats. The walls and floor were coated with smooth cement, and the windows had wooden bars and shutters, but no glass. Near by, another cemented room, with gently sloping floor, represented the latest in Arab bathrooms. Two large earthenware pots filled by the women supplied the water. After five days in the boat without undressing we enjoyed the luxury of a bath.

Rumaliza was a tall, handsome, lithe man, with kindly face and gentlemanly manner, well dressed in embroidered Arab costume with turban. His Ujiji household consisted of two Arab Muscat women, light coloured, fat and unwieldy, who kept much to their own rooms, ten or a dozen handsome, strapping, black wives, each with four to six slaves under her, with other domestic servants. An old slave cook, Atibu, an expert, was told off to wait on us, and two girls were to be always in attendance.

Kiongwe, a Zanzibar Arab who was travelling with Mr. Swann, must have given me a good character, for I was made quite free of the house. Had we stayed only one or two days we should have left with only happy memories of a hospitable visit. But thereafter the constant chatter of sixty to a hundred women in the adjoining court began to pall, while the continuous visits of the principal women to my wife when I was engaged elsewhere became annoying. Inquisitiveness and begging followed, and squabbles and quarrelling outside added to the disquiet.

To us, Rumaliza was always courteous, but when one got glimpses of emaciated slaves in the village, sometimes chained up near a door, and when a slave-raiding band of Rumaliza's ruga-ruga arrived from a raid, the horror of Arab rule was painfully felt. When I spoke to him of the British hatred of slavery, he held that these heathen had no soul and were only beasts.

The arrival of a band of slave-raiders caused no small stir in Ujiji. The slaves, probably on account of our presence, were not with them. The firing of guns, the whiz of bullets, the wild, lulla-boing of the natives, the yelling and excitement of the crowd, were fearsome. Rumaliza counselled us to remain in the house that morning, and closed the gates of the Tembe till the excitement should expend itself. Later in the afternoon the raiders came into the court, a bloodthirsty set of ruffians, with no great goodwill to the white guests.

I suggested to Rumaliza that I should photograph them. They lined up, some aiming dead at me, while I focused the camera. After the picture was taken it gave me somewhat of a scunner when one, down the barrel of whose gun I had been looking five or six yards off, fired it into the air, and we heard the 'ping' of the bullet as it passed over the wall.

Rumaliza had no objection to be photographed but when my wife suggested taking a picture of the black wives, they were frightened and refused. Having no dark room, developing, etc., had to be done by night with a ruby lamp. A number of these wives were sitting chattering when I wished to develop some plates. They were told they could go away when I put out the candle. They remained, but when I blew out the white light and the ruby light showed up there was a yell and they all scrambled for the door and safety! Rushing in on their lord and master, they begged his presence and protection, and he appeared at the door, the frightened women clinging to his skirts. The red light was soon explained, and when next day they recognised a blue print of their lord they too wanted to be taken.

Meanwhile, we had been purchasing ivory. Within a couple of days all the trade goods we had brought had been disposed of to mutual satisfaction and still there remained more ivory to sell. I offered for the balance to give him a letter to our agents in Zanzibar requesting them to pay him so many thousand rupees. Such was the trust he had for the British, that he delivered to me some £2,000 worth of ivory on credit, besides what I paid for in goods.

In Ujiji the native market was better organised than any other I had come across in my travels. Elsewhere one purchased a sheep or goat or ox, but here were booths, with cut joints, etc., neatly laid out for sale. At another place, fish dried or fresh could be bought; another department sold sweet potatoes, pea- nuts, etc., and another tobacco leaves and so on

# CHAPTER XXV

### A NARROW ESCAPE FROM NATIVES

Our ivory purchased, preparations for our return journey began. Most of the dhows were glorified canoes hollowed out of large trees as a foundation. On this were nailed or pinned ribs to which were tied with native cord (not nailed) planks of wood to form the sides. The planks were closely fitted and caulked with cotton soaked in native palm oil, or sometimes with tar. The thwarts, well fastened to the ribs, gave considerable firmness to the structure, the one to which the long heavy mast was fastened being specially strong. It was two such ramshackle boats, about forty feet long by six or seven feet at the widest part that, after much bargaining, we were able to hire to take us back to Abercorn.

Each dhow had one mast twelve or fifteen feet long, and a large lateen sail of strong cotton. There was a small platform at the bow and stern; on the latter, some five feet long by four feet six inches broad, and shaded by an erection, we would have to spend most of our time during the eighteen days and nights journey. A headman and fourteen rowers were engaged for each boat. Our own eight south-country men were divided between the dhows to look after our property.

On Saturday, 19th July 1890, all was ready for departure, our ivory marked, numbered, and shipped, and our boxes stowed away. At that time of year a breeze, often rising to a gale, blows with fair regularity from nine or ten in the forenoon till five or six in the evening. So our journeys had to be by night, no progress worth the exertion entailed being possible in such craft against the day winds. Swann, who was going north in the *Morning Star* started early to take advantage of the breeze, we waited till the afternoon to escape it. We left Ujiji on terms of friendship and satisfaction, even Rumaliza's wives being delighted with what we had given them.

The southerly breeze having at length given place to light airs from the hills, we hoisted our huge lateen sails and sped southward in great comfort. As darkness drew on, we reached the low mouths of the Malagarazi stream, and in the bay came upon dozens of canoes, each with a fire protruding from the bow to attract the fish which were speared or netted. It was a beautiful scene, and for two days and nights we thought we had discovered the very pleasantest mode of travelling.

On the third night, while passing great precipitous mountains coming down sheer into the lake, about 2 a.m. a gale arose from the south against which we could make no headway. The waves were breaking on the rocky shore, and we could not seek shelter there. Holding out from land our men tried to keep the dhow's head to wind, but being unable to do so they dropped their stone (used as anchor), with its long native-made rope, into the deep water, and we rolled about in the trough of the seas. To add to our discomfort and danger the mast-shoe on the bottom of the boat carried loose, and the mast, which was too heavy for the men to unship in such a sea, went crashing from side to side at each roll. Every time she righted herself we felt thankful, but it seemed barely credible that such a boat could longer stand the strain. Yet it did, and when the first reddening of the sky appeared after a terrible night, we were still afloat, and could see the other dhow about half a mile away in much the same condition.

When it was light enough, the men decided to run out with the wind to the middle of the lake and tack back again. But there was no tacking for us that day. Sometimes with bare poles, sometimes with a corner of the sail up, we scudded across a sea of white-crested waves, and did not know what it meant to be free of painful anxiety till about two in the afternoon, when we got to the west coast and into the still waters of a small lagoon in the Uguha country. The wind died completely in the evening, and reluctantly we set sail about midnight. We sailed gently all night and reached another lagoon in the early morning, where we stayed all day and watched the great south waves tearing past us again. We went on in this way for four days. Then the winds lightened and we crossed the lake again, arriving on Saturday morning just a few miles south of the place from which the storm drove us. Again we had to stay in shelter all day, and went on at sunset with the land breezes.

We were now passing the country of the Atongwe, of whom we had been warned as being dangerous and treacherous. The Arabs cited the typical case of a dhow landing and being unheard of for years, when a woman escaping told how all the men had been killed, some women only being spared as slaves. They were considered a kind of Ishmaelites, every man's hand being against them, they reciprocating with interest.

As daylight broke, we passed the rocky entrance to a wide deep bay. The coast-line turned in sharp to the east, and was exposed to the southerly gales. Our course lay nearly south some ten or fifteen miles across the bay, where we hoped we would find shelter in some inlet from the day breeze, clear of the Atongwe country.

While passing the promontory, our attention was attracted to the head of a goat floating on the water. All was going well, the men helping the sails to attain our objective, when about seven o'clock, two hours earlier than usual, the southerly breeze sprang up. We trimmed our sails to keep as far south as possible, and the rowers, in view of the unfriendly beach, plied their oars with goodwill, but as the gale increased it was soon plain we would be driven ashore. With careful steering our dhow got on a mile farther than the other, but a landing was inevitable. With sail lowered and rowing head to wind, we were slowly driven landwards. The shore was rocky, shelving gradually seawards.

As we approached, the crew threw out their stone anchor, and the rowers, jumping overboard in four or five feet of water, held the boat for all they were worth. Then one or two, diving to the anchor-stone, piled over it other stones. To our relief, though the waves were breaking over the boat, our anchor held. Food, bedding, everything damageable, and a little pet monkey (from Ujiji) were carried ashore and we settled down among some bushes clear of the sand to await calmer weather in the evening. After breakfast, as the dhows were still afloat and holding together things looked a little more cheerful.

Then a single native appeared, and we hailed him with perhaps a little more cordiality than was deserved. Giving him a present, we told him we would buy fowls and meal, and soon we were pleased to have a number of not only men but women, a peaceful sign, bartering away and on the best of terms with our party. I sent a present to the chief, who was some miles distant, but to his reiterated request that I should go to his village and see him I had already decided against.

Later, men the worse of beer appeared on the scene, and we had to be still more cautious. During the afternoon the Arab headman of the other dhow, probably to show his importance, gave one or two of the natives a peep at the ivory under his care. Here I may mention what I learned later, that the Atongwe had been preparing to start out on a war raid. Quantities of beer had been made at the chiefs village. A goat had been sacrificed by their medicine men - which explained the head we had seen floating on the lake - and their warriors were ready to start. It was they, who, appearing in the afternoon, disturbed the harmony of the scene. The sight of the ivory, no doubt, also aroused their greed.

About five o'clock we were preparing to dine before embarking, and with all good humour had got the natives sent off that we might eat in peace 'according to our custom.' While dining we kept a sharp look-out along the shore towards the other dhow. We had just finished when we saw natives approaching it. Then there was a commotion, and we heard a gun fired, then another and another. Our natives were making for the boat, covering their retreat with guns. Notwithstanding the heavy waves they got up their anchor and rowed slowly out to sea.

Immediately thereafter a band of armed natives came running towards us. I gave the order to embark our impedimenta. My wife, with our monkey on her shoulder, was carried by two men through the waves to the boat.

When all our boys and the belongings had left the shore, I followed. The men had pulled up the anchor-stone and were getting a move on when the first of the natives arrived, and kneeling on the shore some twenty yards away started firing at us. With my watch in my mouth, the driest place in the circumstances, I reached the dhow neck-deep, but could not, with only one whole arm, pull myself, with soaked clothes, heavy boots, etc. into the boat. Though the men on the shore were firing, my wife leaned over the gunwale to assist me; and she got one of our Mandala natives - Lujanga - to give me a hand. He was immediately shot through the side, the bullet passing out below his shoulder-blade near his spine. Another man then helped me in.

Turning our rifles on our treacherous foes, we soon cleared the beach. Some daring men ran eastward, and manning a big canoe, evidently wished to head us off, but a couple of bullets soon cooled their ardour and they returned.

Rowing out against the gradually diminishing waves, for the gale had subsided, we forgathered with the other dhow. They had escaped without serious casualty. We washed Lujanga's wound and bound him up. We found several bullet-holes through the sides of the dhow; one in our little platform had smashed our biscuit tin. The flat bottom of the dhow, over which the water was rolling, was lumbered with drowned fowls, sleeping-mats, and palm oil, a horrid mess, and there, too, we found Mrs. Moir's terai hat, the disappearance of which she had not noticed. It told its own tale. While leaning out to help me, a bullet had torn open for three inches the outer layer of felt within a quarter of an inch of her forehead and, passing through the double-edge of the brim, had knocked it off into the bottom of the boat. Wet and tired, darkness about us and heaving waters, a sense of horror, mingled with deep thankfulness, came over us as the significance of these marks dawned on us.

Reaching a sheltered cove by daybreak, we kept careful watch all day against surprise, but rested in peace. We both had fever to add to our troubles. There was also sickness among the men. In one case I was horrified to find that one of our Mandala men had small-pox. To put him ashore to be cared for by any native chief would have meant almost certain death to him and a probable epidemic in the country. I therefore had a resting-place arranged for him near the bows, and kept him separate as much as possible from the others.

A few days later, while anchored off a village we found that our heavy rudder, fastened to the hull by strong cords, had been cut away by the native villagers. They had had a quarrel with some one in one of the dhows, or their owners, or relatives, and this was their mode of seeking satisfaction. My wife was lying in fever, but if twenty-four hours were not to be sacrificed, something must be done at once. The natives were frightened to come on board. As they would not discuss the case with any underling, I took my revolver and landed in the pitch darkness, and, after much palaver, appeased their demands in calico, thus redeeming the rudder, which was then refastened, and we proceeded.

After a voyage of eighteen days we reached Abercorn with all our belongings and several tons of ivory, our wounded hero Lujanga decidedly on the mend and our small-pox patient progressing, and ready for a segregation camp. We had accomplished the task we had tackled, had opened trade relations with the principal Tanganyika Arabs, and secured several tons of ivory and incidentally had saved the slaves who would otherwise have been compelled to carry the ivory to the coast. And so, satisfied with our success, we started on the long overland journey to Lake Nyasa.

Not unnaturally, the exceptional exposure and anxiety told on us all, white and black. Mrs. Moir and Lujanga had to be carried in machilas 220 miles to Karonga, whence the *Domira* took us southward. The natives all recovered with rest and feeding. In my case, the malaria seemed to concentrate in a large and painful abscess in my elbowless arm. when this was lanced, I recovered, nor was I again seriously troubled with fever.

In the case of Mrs. Moir, it took the form of recurring low fever, which quickly sapped her strength and brought on a highly critical condition. After some weeks fight for life she was able to accept the kind invitation of Dr. and Mrs. Clement Scott to stay at Blantyre Manse, only a mile from Mandala House, where nursing and kindness assisted convalescence, till in eight weeks she was able to undertake the long journey home. The Shire was then so shallow that the steamer could not come farther up-river than the confluence of the Ruo. We had therefore to travel by boat a long day's journey from Katunga to the Ruo. While waiting at our station for the upcountry mail, which was to follow us overnight, the well-known cry "Ngona!" (crocodile) was raised. I ran, along with the others, to the bank some fifty yards distant, where the natives were gathering. There lay a man's calico and his hoe, there was a splash of water up the bank, nothing more, silence reigned.

The signs were easily read, laying aside his calico the man had entered the river, ankle-deep, and was washing. Stealthily a scaly monster approached under water. When near, it dashed upon him, raising a wave before it. He had but time to cry one word, "Ngona I" when he was seized and carried under water.

Knowing that crocodiles seldom devour their prey at once, a sharp look-out was kept on the river. A crocodile moving about suspiciously was sighted about three hundred yards off, near the other bank, so a boat was sent off manned by willing paddlers andthe body was recovered. As soon as the victim was recognised the death-wail resounded through his village.

The mail and this episode had detained us so long that only by making a very quick run could we hope to reach and sleep on the steamer that night. My wife was still far from well, and she lay in a couch in the stern-sheets. With good paddlers we made swift progress downstream, but twice during the afternoon we were charged by hippopotami, which without warning attacked us in deep water from beneath, trying to drive their great teeth through the bottom. Fortunately, our steel boat was new and strong, so, though their teeth left ominous dents and furrows in the steel, and on the second occasion they nearly capsized us, we escaped with the loss of one paddle, and pushed on to reach the steamer.

As the sun set we were still five or six miles from our destination. We tried to proceed, not withstanding the deep grunts of hippos, which seemed to come from every direction. We knew the river was swarming with crocodiles, and when through the darkness we began to discern the huge bodies of hippos coming out into the shallows for night-feeding, we felt it would be tempting Providence to carry on further. Two things were essential; shallow water so that hippos could not attack from below the boat in which we would sleep and dry ground on which our crew could make fires and cook. We chose a sandbank, mid-river, and breathed more freely when safely moored. Even the mosquitoes that night were a minor discomfort.

We had with us a milk goat for the steamer. It so persisted in pawing the sounding steel of the boat near the prow, that it was put ashore. Frightened by the fires, it ran to the water's edge. Suddenly there was a splash, its bleating ceased, and our goat was gone under the waters, taken by a crocodile.

We slept a troubled sleep while one big hippo bull bellowed to its rival half a mile away, but we did not seek to disturb the crocodiles at this meal.

The very next day we reached the coast and we bade good-bye, seemingly finally, to our work in Africa.

## PROLOGUE

The story of Frederick Moir does not finish when he left Africa in 1892. On his return to Scotland he joined the board of the Africa lakes Company, becoming the Company Secretay in 1911. He attended the negotiations between the Company and the British South Africa Company run by Cecil Rhodes. Rhodes was attempting to take control of the ALC in order to further his ambitions to control the whole of Southern Africa and link with Mackinnon in East Africa.

The truth was that the Africa lakes company were desperate for capital. They had funded, almost entirely without Governmental help, the wars with the Arab slave traders. Rhodes attempted to take advantage and entered into takeover talks. However the morales and motives of the British South Africa company and the African Lakes Company were absolutely poles apart. For Rhodes the raison d'etre for being in business was to make profit and riches, no matter who suffered. For the early pioneers of the lakes company this was an anathema.

The result was the sale of mineral rights in Nyasaland to Rhodes by the ALC (rights which following mining exploration proved to be uneconomical), this raised the necessary finance to stay in business. However the company rejected the complete takeover bid and remained independent.

The African Lakes Company went on to establish a successful network along the the Shire River and the shoreline of Lake Malawi. In the course of the Twentieth Century they moved into hotels, garages and rubber and tobacco plantations amongst many other things. In modern day Malawi, Mandala Limited (the trading name of African Lakes Corporation) employ 3,000 people and are the leading motor company in the area. In many ways what Fred and John Moir helped create is still in existence today.

As for the country he left; In 1891 the area along the Shire and Zambesi Rivers and the West side of the lake, became a British Protectorate known as British Central Africa. In 1907 the area became a colony and was named Nyasaland. This inevitably led to more and more settlers encroaching on native land and traditions. In 1915 there was a violent uprising led by the European-educated Rev John Chilembwe, their main grievance being the large influx of white settlers and its effect on the indigenous farmers. However as with most uprisings in British colonial Africa a compromise was reached and the uprising was squashed.

In 1953, Nyasaland became part of the white controlled, Central African Federation, along with Southern Rhodesia (Zimbabwe) and Northern Rhodesia (Zambia). This federation was finally dissolved in 1963 and a year later independence was granted, with the leader of the Nationalist Malawi Congress Party, Dr Hastings Banda as PM. The country then changed its name to Malawi, but at the same time entered a period of dictatorship under Banda which was to last until 1993.

The travel guides that cover modern day Malawi all have one phrase which is continually repeated. For a country, which has experienced many negative influences in its history, to be described as 'The Warm Heart of Africa' may say something about the contribution of a few Scottish businessmen and the resolution of its people.

Frederick Moir returned to Nyasaland in 1922, by invitation of the African Lakes board. He was feted wherever he went, visting the scenes of the wars and the areas where he had been responsible for the setting up of the trading posts. On his visit he met with many of the natives with whom he had dealt and indeed with many of the children of the chiefs who were now in positions of authority themselves. For many of them 'Chindevu' had been a part of their liberation from slavery.

John Moir stayed on in the area and was rewarded for his work for the Company with a large farm in the Shire Highlands. Here he worked for many years before retiring back to the old country. Interestingly he became deeply involved in Beekeeping at at the time of his death in 1940, was accepted to have the 'largest collection of beekeping books in the Empire'(Entry in Who was Who)

Moir returned to Scotland and set about his memoirs, published in 1925 by Hodder and Stoughton entitles 'After Livingstone. An African Trade Romance', on which this book is based. It is surely evident that the subtitle for his book goes a long way to describe his relationship with the continent of Africa.

*Frederick Moir*